MW01537363

The Perfected Paris

A Traveler's Companion Through the City of Lights

By

Glory .G. Michael

Table of Contents

Practicalities

Index

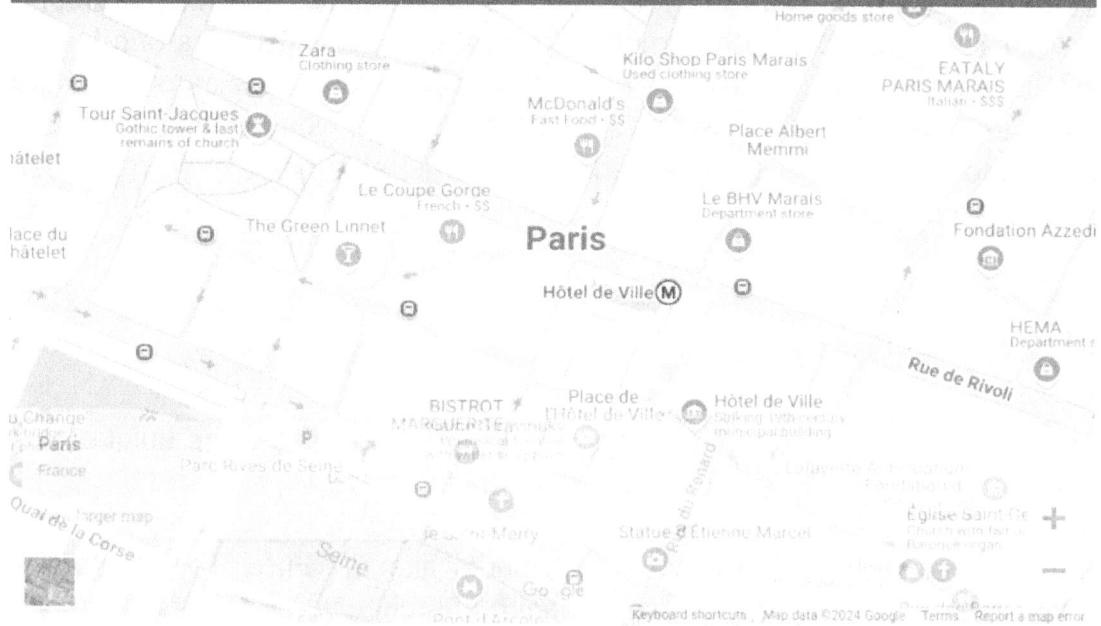

HOW TO SCAN

1. Open the camera app on your phone.

2. Point the camera at the QR code.

3. Ensure the QR code is within the viewfinder.

4. Wait for the notification or link to appear.

5. Tap the notification or link.

6. Follow the link or access the content associated with the QR code.

Introduction

Paris, often referred to as the "City of Light," is a destination that inspires countless dreams and adventures. With its timeless charm, world-class art, historic landmarks, and exquisite cuisine, it's no surprise that Paris consistently ranks as one of the most visited cities in the world. This travel guide will equip you with all the essential information to make your Parisian experience unforgettable, whether you're a first-time visitor or a seasoned traveler.

Why Paris?

Paris is more than just a city; it's an experience. Its allure lies in its unique ability to combine historical grandeur with a modern, vibrant lifestyle.

Art and Architecture: Home to iconic landmarks like the Eiffel Tower, Notre-Dame Cathedral, and the Louvre, Paris boasts a wealth of architectural wonders. The city's art scene is unparalleled, with museums and galleries housing masterpieces from every era.

Cultural Heritage: Paris is synonymous with romance, fashion, and intellectual thought. From the Enlightenment to the fashion runways, Paris has shaped global culture and continues to do so.

Cuisine: Whether it's the buttery croissants, creamy cheeses, or decadent desserts, Paris offers a gastronomic journey that's second to none. Its cafés, bistros, and Michelin-starred restaurants cater to every palate.

Atmosphere: Strolling along the Seine, sipping coffee at a sidewalk café, or watching the city light up at night evokes a sense of magic that is uniquely Parisian.

Overview of Parisian Culture

Parisian culture is deeply rooted in history, art, and a joie de vivre (joy of living) that permeates every aspect of life.

The Parisian Way of Life: Parisians prioritize balance and beauty in their daily lives. Meals are savored slowly, conversation is an art, and time is taken to appreciate the finer details of life.

Art and Literature: Paris has long been a hub for creatives, attracting artists, writers, and thinkers. From Monet to Hemingway, the city's streets have inspired some of the world's greatest minds.

Fashion Capital: Known as the fashion capital of the world, Paris sets global trends with its haute couture shows and chic street style.

Celebrations and Traditions: Parisian festivals, like Bastille Day and Nuit Blanche, showcase the city's vibrant spirit. Daily rituals, such as shopping at local markets or enjoying an evening apéro (pre-dinner drink), are equally significant.

When to Visit Paris

The best time to visit Paris depends on your interests and tolerance for crowds and weather.

Spring (March to May): Paris blooms in spring, making it ideal for outdoor activities like strolling through gardens and exploring the city on foot. Temperatures are mild, and the city is alive with events and festivals.

Summer (June to August): Warm weather and extended daylight make summer popular for sightseeing and evening outings. However, expect larger crowds and higher prices.

Autumn (September to November): Fall brings cooler weather, fewer tourists, and vibrant foliage. It's an excellent time for art lovers, as many exhibitions open in the autumn months.

Winter (December to February): Though chilly, winter in Paris is enchanting. The holiday season transforms the city with lights, markets, and festivities. Indoor attractions like museums are less crowded.

Getting to Paris: Flights, Trains, and Other Options

Paris is one of Europe's most accessible cities, with numerous options for getting there:

Flights:
Paris is served by two major airports: Charles de Gaulle (CDG) and Orly (ORY). CDG handles most international flights, while ORY is popular for domestic and European travel. A third airport, Beauvais (BVA), caters to budget airlines but is farther from the city. From the airport, you can reach central Paris by RER train, bus, or taxi.

Trains:
Paris is well-connected by high-speed trains. The Eurostar links London to Paris in about 2.5 hours, while the Thalys connects Brussels and Amsterdam. France's extensive TGV network also makes Paris accessible from cities like Lyon, Bordeaux, and Marseille.

Driving:
If you prefer road trips, Paris is reachable by car from neighboring European countries. However, parking and traffic in the city can be challenging.

Buses:
Long-distance buses are a budget-friendly option. Companies like FlixBus and BlaBlaCar Bus connect Paris with major cities across Europe.

Paris Essentials: Language, Currency, and Tipping

Language:
French is the official language, and while many Parisians speak English, learning a few basic phrases can go a long way in enhancing your experience. Simple greetings like "Bonjour" (Good morning) and "Merci" (Thank you) are appreciated.

Currency:
Paris uses the Euro (€). ATMs are widely available, and credit cards are accepted almost everywhere. Carrying some cash for small purchases is still a good idea.

Tipping:
Service charges are included in restaurant bills, but rounding up or leaving small change is customary if you're satisfied with the service. For taxis, rounding up to the nearest euro is standard. In hotels, tipping porters and housekeeping staff a few euros is appreciated.

Historic Paris Walk

The historic heart of Paris offers a journey through centuries of history, culture, and architectural splendor. This walk takes you through the essence of Paris, starting at its ancient core on Île de la Cité, passing the grandeur of Notre-Dame Cathedral, meandering through the intellectual charm of the Latin Quarter, and uncovering hidden gems along the Seine.

Discovering Île de la Cité

Île de la Cité, the cradle of Paris, is where the city began over 2,000 years ago. This small island on the Seine holds some of the most iconic landmarks and offers a perfect starting point for your walk.

Historical Significance:
As the original settlement of the Parisii tribe, the island has witnessed the transformation of Paris from a Roman outpost to a global metropolis.

Sights to See:

Palais de Justice: A striking building that has been a center of judicial power for centuries.

Sainte-Chapelle: Known for its stunning stained-glass windows, this Gothic masterpiece is a must-visit. The intricate panes depict biblical stories in vivid, jewel-like colors.

Pont Neuf: Despite its name meaning "New Bridge," this is the oldest standing bridge in Paris, offering beautiful views of the Seine.

Place Dauphine: A peaceful square tucked away on the western tip of the island, perfect for a quiet respite.

Tips for Exploring:
Early mornings are ideal to enjoy the tranquility of the island before the crowds arrive.

Don't miss the charming bookstalls along the Seine nearby, where you can find vintage books and artwork.

Notre-Dame Cathedral Highlights

An icon of Gothic architecture, the Notre-Dame Cathedral has stood proudly on Île de la Cité since the 12th century. While the 2019 fire damaged parts of the cathedral, it remains a testament to human creativity and resilience.

Architectural Marvels:

The Facade: Admire the intricate details of the West Facade, including its rose window, gargoyles, and sculptures depicting biblical scenes.

The Towers: Though climbing is temporarily unavailable, the twin towers remain iconic symbols of Paris, offering stunning views from the outside.

Flying Buttresses: Walk around the back to see the remarkable flying buttresses that support the cathedral's weight.

Spiritual Significance:
Step inside to experience the cathedral's serene interior. The stained-glass windows, including the South Rose Window, create a kaleidoscope of colors when sunlight streams through.

Nearby Attractions:

Square Jean XXIII: A charming garden behind the cathedral where you can relax and admire the architecture.

Crypte Archéologique: An underground museum showcasing the remnants of Paris' Roman roots, located right in front of the cathedral.

The Latin Quarter Stroll

Just across the Seine from Notre-Dame, the Latin Quarter is a lively district steeped in history, intellect, and bohemian charm. It's named for the Latin-speaking students who once frequented its streets during the Middle Ages.

What to See:

Sorbonne University: One of Europe's oldest and most prestigious universities. Its historic buildings are worth a look.

Panthéon: This neoclassical mausoleum honors France's greatest figures, including Voltaire, Rousseau, and Marie Curie.

Rue Mouffetard: A bustling street lined with shops, cafés, and market stalls, offering a slice of local Parisian life.

Atmosphere:
The Latin Quarter is perfect for wandering without a plan. Its narrow cobblestone streets, vibrant bookstores, and quaint cafés create an ambiance that's both energetic and timeless.

Cultural Highlights:

Shakespeare and Company: A legendary English-language bookstore and literary haven for writers like Hemingway and Fitzgerald.

Jardin des Plantes: A serene botanical garden where you can take a break from the urban buzz.

Hidden Gems Along the Seine

The Seine River is the lifeblood of Paris, and walking along its banks reveals a mix of iconic sights and hidden treasures.

Booksellers and Bouquinistes:
Along the quays, you'll find green-painted boxes filled with vintage books, posters, and souvenirs. These booksellers have been a Parisian tradition since the 16th century.

The Square du Vert-Galant:
Located at the tip of Île de la Cité, this small park offers a tranquil spot to sit and watch boats pass by on the river.

Love Lock Bridge:
While the original Pont des Arts locks were removed, the sentiment remains, and couples often leave tokens of their love here.

Pont Alexandre III:
Though farther along the Seine, this bridge is worth visiting for its lavish decorations and views of the Eiffel Tower.

River Cruises:
A Seine cruise offers a unique perspective of Paris, especially at night when landmarks like the Eiffel Tower and Louvre are illuminated. Opt for a smaller boat for a more intimate experience.

This Historic Paris Walk combines history, culture, and romance, offering an unforgettable introduction to the city's essence. Each stop along the way provides a deeper understanding of Paris' past and its enduring beauty.

Louvre Tour

The Louvre Museum, or Musée du Louvre, is the crown jewel of Parisian culture and one of the most renowned art museums in the world. A visit to the Louvre is more than a museum tour; it's an immersion into thousands of years of human creativity. Whether you're an art connoisseur or a casual visitor, the Louvre offers an unforgettable experience.

Louvre , museum

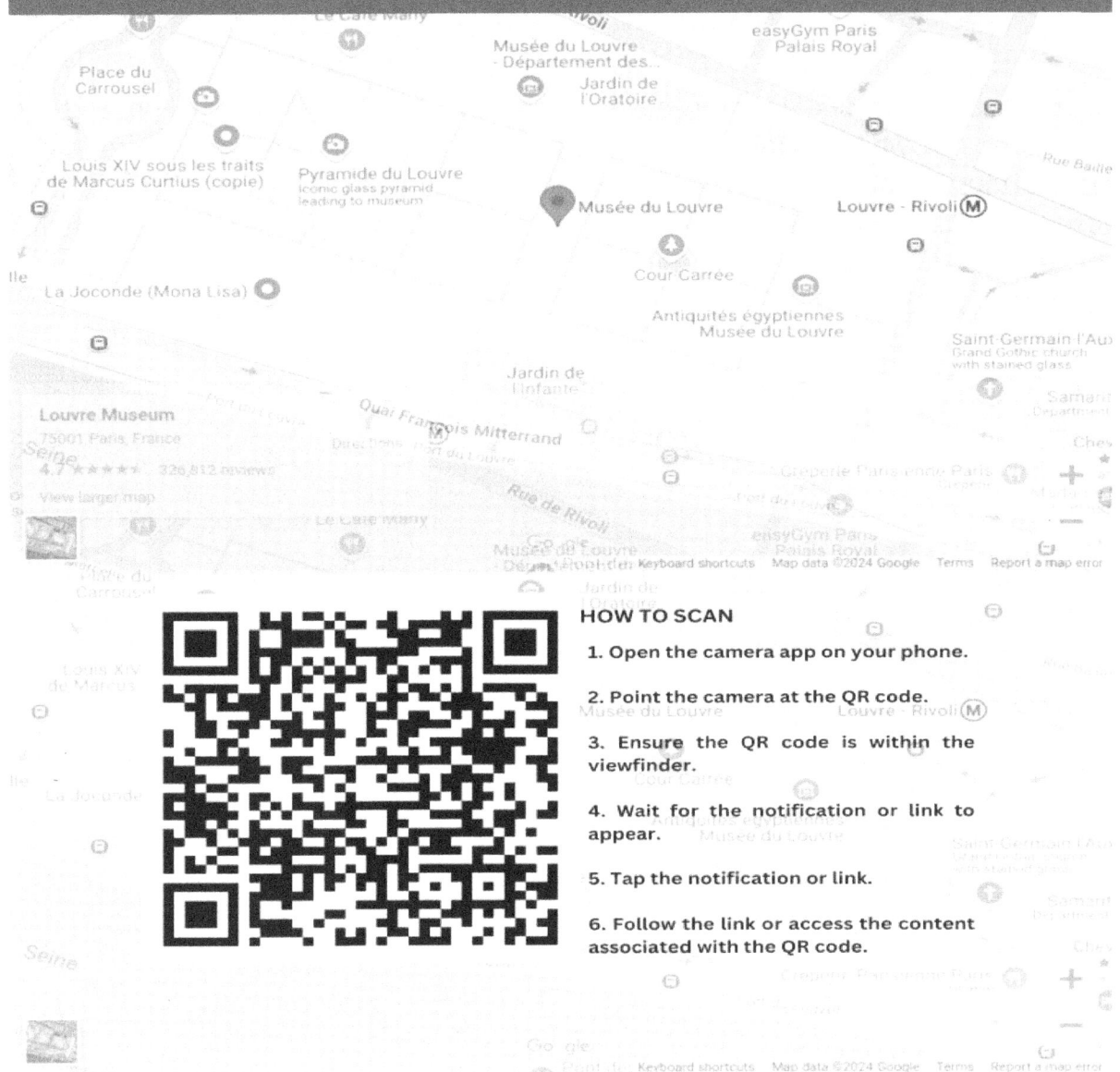

HOW TO SCAN

1. Open the camera app on your phone.

2. Point the camera at the QR code.

3. Ensure the QR code is within the viewfinder.

4. Wait for the notification or link to appear.

5. Tap the notification or link.

6. Follow the link or access the content associated with the QR code.

A Brief History of the Louvre

The story of the Louvre is as fascinating as the masterpieces it houses. From a medieval fortress to the largest museum on Earth, the Louvre's evolution mirrors the history of Paris itself.

Medieval Beginnings (12th–16th Centuries):
The Louvre was originally constructed as a fortress by King Philip II in 1190 to protect Paris from invasion. Remnants of this medieval structure, including the original moat and foundation, can still be seen in the museum's lower levels.

By the 16th century, King Francis I transformed the fortress into a royal residence. It was during this period that Francis acquired Leonardo da Vinci's "Mona Lisa", laying the foundation for what would become one of the world's greatest art collections.

The Louvre as a Royal Palace (16th–17th Centuries):
Subsequent monarchs, including Catherine de' Medici and Louis XIV, expanded the Louvre into a sprawling palace. Its stunning architecture, such as the Cour Carrée and the Tuileries Gardens, reflects the grandeur of French royalty.

Louis XIV eventually moved his court to Versailles, leaving the Louvre primarily for artistic and academic purposes.

Birth of a Museum (18th Century):
The idea of a public museum began to take shape during the Enlightenment. In 1793, during the French Revolution, the Louvre was officially opened as the Muséum Central des Arts. The revolutionary government seized royal and church collections, enriching the museum's holdings.

19th and 20th Century Expansion:
Napoleon Bonaparte greatly expanded the Louvre's collection, including treasures looted from his campaigns. His contributions earned the museum the temporary name Musée Napoléon.

The Louvre underwent significant renovations in the 19th and 20th centuries, adding new wings and galleries. Major acquisitions, such as the Venus de Milo and the Winged Victory of Samothrace, further solidified its global reputation.

Modern Era and the Pyramid (1989):
The most striking modern addition to the Louvre is the glass pyramid designed by Chinese-American architect I. M. Pei. Initially controversial, the pyramid now serves as the museum's main entrance and a symbol of the Louvre's seamless blend of tradition and innovation.

What to See on a Louvre Tour

With over 35,000 artworks on display, planning your visit is essential. The museum is divided into three main wings: Denon, Richelieu, and Sully. Here are some highlights:

1. The Denon Wing:

Mona Lisa: The star of the Louvre, Leonardo da Vinci's enigmatic portrait draws millions each year.

The Wedding at Cana: Opposite the Mona Lisa, this massive painting by Veronese depicts a biblical feast with incredible detail.

The Winged Victory of Samothrace: A stunning Greek sculpture of Nike, the goddess of victory, perched dramatically on a staircase.

The Raft of the Medusa: A powerful Romantic-era painting by Géricault that captures a moment of tragedy and heroism.

2. The Richelieu Wing:

Napoleon III Apartments: These opulent rooms offer a glimpse into 19th-century royal luxury.

Code of Hammurabi: One of the oldest written legal codes in the world, dating back to ancient Mesopotamia.

Sculptures Courtyards: Featuring works like Michelangelo's "Dying Slave" and "Rebellious Slave."

3. The Sully Wing:

Venus de Milo: A timeless representation of beauty and one of the most famous Greek sculptures.

Egyptian Antiquities: A fascinating collection of mummies, statues, and artifacts from ancient Egypt.

Medieval Louvre: Explore the remains of the original fortress beneath the museum.

Tips for Navigating the Louvre

1. Plan Ahead:

Purchase tickets online to skip the lines.

Decide which wings or artworks you want to prioritize; it's impossible to see everything in one day.

2. Timing:

Early mornings and late afternoons are less crowded.

Wednesday and Friday evenings offer extended hours for a quieter experience.

3. Guided Tours and Apps:

Consider a guided tour or an audio guide to gain deeper insights into the artwork. The Louvre also has its own app to help you navigate.

4. Comfort:

Wear comfortable shoes, as the museum spans 72,735 square meters of exhibition space.

Take breaks in the museum's cafés or the Tuileries Gardens.

5. Photography:

Photography is allowed in most areas but without flash. Be mindful of your surroundings and avoid obstructing other visitors.

A visit to the Louvre is a journey through human history and creativity, offering something for every type of traveler. Whether you're drawn to ancient artifacts, Renaissance masterpieces, or the palace's architectural splendor, the Louvre will leave you inspired and in awe. Let me know if you'd like a detailed itinerary for exploring the museum!

Must-See Masterpieces at the Louvre

With its vast collection of over 35,000 artworks spanning centuries and continents, the Louvre houses some of the most iconic and celebrated masterpieces in the world. To help you make the most of your visit, here are the absolute must-see highlights across its three main wings: Denon, Richelieu, and Sully.

1. Denon Wing Highlights

The Denon Wing is home to some of the Louvre's most famous artworks, including Renaissance masterpieces and monumental paintings.

Mona Lisa (La Gioconda):
By Leonardo da Vinci, this enigmatic portrait is the museum's biggest draw. Its mysterious smile and the subject's gaze have captivated viewers for centuries. Despite its small size, the Mona Lisa commands the largest crowds in the Louvre.

The Wedding at Cana:
Painted by Paolo Veronese, this massive canvas depicts Christ's first miracle, turning water into wine. The vivid colors and bustling scene make it a breathtaking companion to the Mona Lisa, displayed just opposite.

The Winged Victory of Samothrace:
This ancient Greek sculpture of Nike, the goddess of victory, exudes movement and drama. Perched atop a staircase, it's one of the most visually striking pieces in the

museum.

The Coronation of Napoleon:
Jacques-Louis David's masterpiece captures Napoleon's self-coronation in Notre-Dame Cathedral. The painting is notable for its immense scale and detailed depiction of power and opulence.

Liberty Leading the People:
Eugène Delacroix's iconic painting is a symbol of revolution and freedom. Marianne, the personification of Liberty, leads a charge with the French tricolor flag.

2. Richelieu Wing Highlights

The Richelieu Wing focuses on sculptures, royal artifacts, and treasures from around the world.

Napoleon III Apartments:
A must-see for lovers of luxury, these rooms provide a glimpse into 19th-century French opulence. The gilded chandeliers, lavish furnishings, and intricate decor are breathtaking.

Code of Hammurabi:
An ancient Babylonian artifact, this basalt stele contains one of the oldest written legal codes. It's a significant piece for understanding early law and governance.

Sculptures Courtyard:
Highlights include Michelangelo's Rebellious Slave and Dying Slave, showcasing the artist's masterful understanding of human form and emotion.

The Victory Stele of Naram-Sin:
This Akkadian artifact from ancient Mesopotamia celebrates a military triumph and provides a fascinating glimpse into early art and storytelling.

3. Sully Wing Highlights

The Sully Wing is the oldest section of the Louvre, focusing on classical antiquities and ancient art.

Venus de Milo:
This Greek statue, believed to depict Aphrodite, the goddess of love, is an enduring symbol of beauty and grace.

The Seated Scribe:
A fascinating piece from ancient Egypt, this lifelike sculpture of a scribe is notable for its attentive expression and vibrant colors.

The Great Sphinx of Tanis:
One of the largest sphinxes outside of Egypt, this colossal statue is an impressive testament to ancient Egyptian craftsmanship.

The Lamassu:
These winged, human-headed bulls from Assyrian civilization once guarded palace gates, symbolizing power and protection.

Medieval Louvre:
Beneath the Sully Wing lies the museum's oldest section: the remains of the original medieval fortress built by King Philip II.

Tips for Navigating the Museum

The Louvre can be overwhelming due to its size and sheer number of exhibits. Use these tips to ensure a smooth and enjoyable visit:

1. Plan Your Visit

Buy Tickets in Advance:
Purchase skip-the-line tickets online to avoid long queues. Booking a time slot ensures a hassle-free entry.

Know Your Priorities:
Decide which wings or artworks you want to see in advance. It's impossible to see everything in one visit, so focus on the masterpieces or specific collections of interest.

Time It Right:
The museum is busiest from late morning to mid-afternoon. Opt for early morning or evening visits, especially on Wednesdays and Fridays when the museum has extended hours.

2. Navigate Efficiently

Use a Map:
Grab a museum map at the entrance or download the Louvre's official app to help you find specific artworks and galleries.

Follow a Themed Tour:
The Louvre offers themed trails, such as "Masterpieces" or "Ancient Egypt." These can guide you through highlights in an organized way.

Stay Grounded:
Focus on one or two wings instead of trying to cover the entire museum. This prevents exhaustion and allows you to appreciate the art fully.

3. Comfort and Accessibility

Dress Comfortably:
Wear comfortable shoes, as you'll be walking and standing for hours. Lightweight clothing and a small bag are recommended.

Take Breaks:
The Louvre has several cafés and rest areas. A quick stop for coffee or a snack can refresh your energy for the next gallery.

Accessibility:
The museum is wheelchair accessible, and elevators are available for visitors with mobility challenges.

4. Enhance Your Experience

Guided Tours:
Join a guided tour to learn fascinating details about the artworks and the museum's history. Private tours can offer an even deeper dive into specific collections.

Audio Guides:
Rent an audio guide or use the Louvre's app for detailed explanations about major exhibits.

Photography:
Photography without flash is allowed in most areas. Be respectful of other visitors when taking pictures.

5. Stay Organized

Start with the Highlights:
Begin with the Denon Wing's masterpieces, as they draw the largest crowds. Visiting early ensures you'll have a better view.

Travel Light:
Large bags and luggage aren't allowed, but there are lockers available for storage.

Keep Your Ticket Handy:
You may need to show your ticket multiple times, especially when entering different wings.

The Louvre is a treasure trove of human creativity, and proper planning ensures you can experience its wonders without feeling overwhelmed. Whether you're marveling at the Mona Lisa or discovering lesser-known gems, the museum promises a journey you'll never forget. Let me know if you'd like a suggested itinerary or additional tips!

Exploring the Cour Napoléon and Glass Pyramid

The Cour Napoléon, or Napoleon's Courtyard, is the grand entrance to the Louvre

Museum and one of Paris's most iconic landmarks. At its heart stands the striking Glass Pyramid, an architectural marvel that has become synonymous with the Louvre itself. This area is not just a gateway to one of the world's greatest museums but also a masterpiece of design and innovation that blends modernity with history.

The Cour Napoléon: A Historical Overview

The Cour Napoléon is part of the larger Louvre Palace complex, which has evolved from a medieval fortress to a Renaissance royal residence, and finally, into the world-renowned museum it is today. Named after Emperor Napoleon III, who expanded the Louvre during the 19th century, the courtyard is surrounded by ornate facades showcasing classical French architecture.

Architectural Highlights:
The buildings encircling the courtyard feature intricate carvings, majestic columns, and statues of significant historical figures. These facades provide a glimpse into France's royal and imperial past.

Symbol of Transition:
The Cour Napoléon reflects the Louvre's transformation from a royal palace to a public space of learning and art, making it a powerful symbol of cultural openness.

The Glass Pyramid: A Modern Icon

The Glass Pyramid, designed by Chinese-American architect I. M. Pei, was inaugurated in 1989 amidst much controversy. Over time, it has become a beloved symbol of the Louvre and modern Parisian design.

Architectural Design:
The pyramid is composed of 673 panes of glass and stands 21.6 meters (71 feet) tall. Its minimalist geometric design contrasts with the surrounding classical architecture, creating a harmonious blend of old and new.

Functionality:
Beyond its beauty, the pyramid serves as the museum's main entrance. Visitors descend through it into a spacious underground lobby that connects the Louvre's three wings: Denon, Sully, and Richelieu.

Cultural Significance:
Initially met with skepticism, the Glass Pyramid is now celebrated as a bold architectural statement, symbolizing the Louvre's commitment to innovation while honoring its historical roots.

Key Features to Explore in the Cour Napoléon

The Inverted Pyramid:
Inside the underground lobby, near the main entrance, lies the Inverted Pyramid, a smaller glass structure pointing downwards. It's a fascinating complement to the main pyramid and a favorite spot for photographs.

Fountains and Reflective Pools:
Surrounding the Glass Pyramid are elegant fountains and shallow pools, which provide a serene ambiance. On sunny days, the water reflects the pyramid and the historic buildings, creating stunning visuals.

Statues and Sculptures:
The courtyard features several statues that add to its grandeur, including equestrian statues and other classical works that honor French history.

Tips for Enjoying the Cour Napoléon and Pyramid

1. Visit at Different Times of Day:

Daytime: Marvel at the interplay of sunlight on the glass and surrounding architecture.

Nighttime: The pyramid is illuminated after dark, creating a magical glow that highlights its beauty and makes for incredible photos.

2. Capture Stunning Photos:

For fewer crowds, visit early in the morning or late in the evening. The symmetrical design of the courtyard and pyramid creates perfect opportunities for architectural photography.

3. Explore the Underground Lobby:

The lobby beneath the pyramid offers a modern and spacious entry point to the museum, complete with ticket counters, shops, and cafes.

4. Combine History and Modernity:

Spend time appreciating the juxtaposition of classical and modern styles. Take a moment to study the intricate details of the palace facades, then contrast them with the clean lines of the pyramid.

The Cour Napoléon and Glass Pyramid are more than just a passage to the Louvre; they are an experience in their own right. They represent the dynamic spirit of Paris, where history and innovation coexist harmoniously. Whether you're a first-time visitor or a seasoned traveler, this space will leave you inspired and ready to delve into the treasures of the Louvre Museum.

Orsay Museum Tour

The Orsay: From Train Station to Art Haven

The Musée d'Orsay, located on the left bank of the Seine, is one of Paris's most beloved art museums, housing a world-class collection of 19th- and early 20th-century art. Its story, however, begins not as a cultural institution but as a magnificent train station built for the 1900 Paris Exposition Universelle (World's Fair).

The Origins: Gare d'Orsay

Design and Construction:
The Gare d'Orsay was designed by architect Victor Laloux and completed in 1900. Its elegant Beaux-Arts façade, with ornate stonework and a clock tower, complemented the grandeur of the surrounding city. The station featured state-of-the-art technology for its time, including electrified tracks, and was a hub for trains arriving from southwestern France.

A Symbol of Modernity:
As a showpiece for the 1900 World's Fair, the Gare d'Orsay symbolized France's industrial and artistic achievements. Its spacious design and innovative use of glass and metal embodied the era's optimism and progress.

The Decline of the Train Station

Changes in Transportation:
By the 1930s, the Gare d'Orsay's platforms had become too short for newer, longer trains. Its significance as a railway hub diminished, and by 1939, it ceased serving long-distance travel.

Repurposing the Space:
After its closure as a train station, the building found temporary uses, including as a

postal center during World War II and a set for films like Orson Welles's "The Trial" in the 1960s. Despite its declining utility, the building's architectural beauty sparked debates about its preservation.

The Transformation into a Museum

The Vision:
In the 1970s, the French government decided to repurpose the Gare d'Orsay into a museum dedicated to art from 1848 to 1914, bridging the gap between the collections of the Louvre and the modern art displayed at the Centre Pompidou.

Restoration and Redesign:
Architects Gae Aulenti, Victor Laloux, and others led the transformation, retaining much of the original structure while creating modern exhibition spaces. The station's grand central hall was repurposed into a soaring gallery for sculptures, while smaller galleries were added for paintings and decorative arts.

Opening to the Public:
The Musée d'Orsay officially opened in 1986, instantly garnering acclaim for its innovative design and extraordinary collection. The building's rebirth symbolized a perfect harmony of history and modernity.

Architectural Highlights

The museum's architecture is a masterpiece in itself and deserves attention as much as the art within:

The Great Hall:
The former train platform now serves as the museum's central exhibition space. The soaring ceilings, arched windows, and monumental clock create a dramatic setting for sculptures and installations.

The Clocks:
The two giant clocks on the museum's façade and interior offer stunning views of the Seine and Paris. These clocks are relics of the building's railway past and have become iconic symbols of the Musée d'Orsay.

Glass and Light:
The use of glass in the ceiling and large windows floods the interior with natural light, enhancing the viewing experience and paying homage to the building's original design.

A Home for Masterpieces

The transformation of the Gare d'Orsay into a museum not only preserved an architectural treasure but also gave it a new purpose. Today, the Musée d'Orsay is home to:

Impressionist and Post-Impressionist Works:
The museum's collection of masterpieces by artists like Monet, Van Gogh, Degas, and Renoir is unparalleled.

Sculptures and Decorative Arts:
Works by Rodin, Carpeaux, and others are displayed in the central hall, while exquisite Art Nouveau furniture and objects are showcased in side galleries.

Temporary Exhibitions:
The museum regularly hosts themed exhibitions, bringing fresh perspectives to its collection and attracting art lovers from around the world.

Why Visit the Musée d'Orsay?

The Musée d'Orsay is more than just a repository of art; it is a testament to Paris's commitment to preserving and celebrating its cultural heritage. The building's journey from an industrial marvel to an artistic haven mirrors the evolution of Paris itself—a city that seamlessly blends the past and the present.

For visitors, the museum offers a chance to explore not only incredible art but also the enduring legacy of one of Paris's most iconic landmarks. Let me know if you'd like more details about the museum's highlights or tips for visiting!

Iconic Works and Artists at the Musée d'Orsay

The Musée d'Orsay boasts an unparalleled collection of works by some of the most celebrated artists of the 19th and early 20th centuries. Its focus on Impressionism and Post-Impressionism makes it a haven for art enthusiasts. Here's a closer look at the most iconic works and artists you can't miss:

Claude Monet (1840–1926)

Monet, the father of Impressionism, is well-represented at the museum with several of his masterpieces.

"La Rue Montorgueil"
This festive painting captures the vibrant celebration of the French national holiday, with fluttering flags and a lively atmosphere.

"Women in the Garden"
An earlier work that showcases Monet's fascination with light and outdoor settings.

Vincent van Gogh (1853–1890)

Van Gogh's intense and emotional works are a highlight of the museum.

"Starry Night Over the Rhône"
This stunning painting of Arles' night sky reflects his mastery of color and light.

"Self-Portrait"
One of Van Gogh's many self-portraits, this piece provides a haunting glimpse into the artist's turbulent psyche.

Edgar Degas (1834–1917)

Known for his depictions of dancers, Degas's works capture movement and grace.

"The Ballet Class"
A quintessential Degas painting that shows ballerinas practicing under their teacher's watchful eye.

"The Little Dancer of Fourteen Years"
This bronze sculpture is an iconic representation of his fascination with ballet.

Édouard Manet (1832–1883)

Manet bridged realism and Impressionism, challenging artistic conventions of his time.

"The Luncheon on the Grass"
A provocative and groundbreaking work that redefined modern art.

"Olympia"
A portrait of a reclining nude woman that shocked 19th-century audiences for its bold realism.

Auguste Renoir (1841–1919)

Renoir's works are celebrated for their warm tones and joyous scenes.

"Dance at Le Moulin de la Galette"
This painting captures the lively atmosphere of a Parisian dance hall, filled with light and movement.

"The Bathers"
A later work that reflects Renoir's fascination with the human form.

Gustave Courbet (1819–1877)

Courbet's realist works laid the foundation for modern art.

"The Origin of the World"
A daring piece that explores themes of life and creation.

"A Burial at Ornans"
A monumental work that depicts a rural funeral in a raw and realistic manner.

Georges Seurat (1859–1891)

Seurat's pointillism revolutionized the art of painting.

"The Circus"
A vibrant and detailed portrayal of a bustling circus scene.

"A Sunday Afternoon on the Island of La Grande Jatte" (study)
A precursor to his masterpiece, showcasing his technique and vision.

Camille Pissarro (1830–1903)

Pissarro's landscapes and cityscapes are a vital part of the Impressionist movement.

"The Boulevard Montmartre at Night"
This work showcases Pissarro's ability to capture urban life with depth and atmosphere.

Special Exhibits and Rotating Collections

The Musée d'Orsay is not just about its permanent collection. Its special exhibits and rotating collections offer visitors a chance to explore new perspectives and themes.

Themes of Special Exhibits

1. Artist Retrospectives:
Past exhibits have focused on individual artists such as Berthe Morisot, Paul Gauguin, and Van Gogh, providing deeper insights into their lives and works.

2. Art Movements:

Temporary exhibits often explore specific movements like Symbolism, Pointillism, or Art Nouveau, highlighting their significance within the broader context of art history.

3. Cultural Intersections:
Exhibits sometimes delve into the influence of other cultures on French art, such as Japanese prints or African art.

Recent Notable Exhibitions

"Picasso: Blue and Rose Periods"
This exhibit explored Picasso's early works, showcasing the emotional depth of his Blue Period and the softer tones of his Rose Period.

"The Impressionists in London"
Highlighting works created by Impressionist artists during their time in England, it offered a fresh perspective on their creative journeys.

"Black Models: From Géricault to Matisse"
An exploration of the representation of Black figures in French art from the 19th and early 20th centuries.

Why Explore Rotating Collections?

1. Diversity of Perspectives:
These exhibits bring lesser-known artists and movements to the forefront, enriching your understanding of art history.

2. Exclusive Works:
Many temporary exhibits include works on loan from other prestigious museums and private collections.

3. Engaging Themes:
The museum curates thought-provoking exhibits that often tie historical art to contemporary issues.

Tips for Visiting Special Exhibits

Book Tickets in Advance: Popular exhibits often sell out, so secure your spot early.

Visit During Off-Peak Hours: Arrive early or late in the day to avoid crowds.

Use Guided Tours: Many exhibits offer guided tours or audio guides tailored to the exhibit's theme.

The Musée d'Orsay's combination of iconic masterpieces and dynamic temporary exhibits ensures that every visit feels fresh, offering something new to discover every time.

Café and Gift Shop Recommendations at the Musée d'Orsay

A visit to the Musée d'Orsay isn't complete without pausing to enjoy its charming cafés and exploring its well-curated gift shops. Whether you're looking for a delicious meal, a quick coffee break, or a memorable souvenir, the museum offers excellent options.

Café Recommendations

1. Café Campana

Location: On the fifth floor, near the iconic clock.

Atmosphere: Designed by the Campana brothers, this café combines Art Nouveau aesthetics with a modern touch, making it a perfect spot for art and design enthusiasts.

Menu Highlights:

Light meals such as quiches, salads, and sandwiches.

Delectable desserts, including tarts and pastries.

A selection of fine French wines and coffee.

Why Visit:

The large clock window offers a breathtaking view of Paris, including Montmartre and the Sacré-Cœur Basilica.

It's an Instagram-worthy spot for photos!

2. Restaurant du Musée d'Orsay

Location: On the first floor, in the former ballroom of the Orsay railway station.

Atmosphere: Luxurious and elegant, with grand chandeliers, gold accents, and opulent decor reminiscent of the Belle Époque.

Menu Highlights:

Full-course meals featuring traditional French cuisine, such as duck confit, foie gras, and crème brûlée.

Vegetarian and children's menu options are also available.

Why Visit:

Perfect for a leisurely lunch or special occasion dining.

You'll feel like you've stepped into a bygone era while enjoying exquisite food.

3. Café de l'Ours

Location: Ground floor, near the museum entrance.

Atmosphere: Casual and family-friendly, ideal for a quick snack or drink.

Menu Highlights:

Fresh pastries, sandwiches, and salads.

A variety of beverages, including coffee, tea, and soft drinks.

Why Visit:

Convenient for a quick refreshment before or after your museum visit.

Less crowded than the other dining options.

Gift Shop Recommendations

The Musée d'Orsay has two main gift shops, offering a wide array of items inspired by the museum's collection and the art movements it represents.

1. Main Gift Shop

Location: Ground floor, near the main entrance.

What You'll Find:

Art Books: Catalogs of current and past exhibitions, as well as books on Impressionism and Post-Impressionism.

Reproductions: High-quality prints and posters of masterpieces by Van Gogh, Monet, and Renoir.

Stationery: Beautiful notebooks, calendars, and postcards featuring iconic artworks.

Jewelry and Accessories: Elegant pieces inspired by Art Nouveau designs.

Why Visit:

A comprehensive collection of souvenirs for art lovers.

Ideal for thoughtful gifts or personal keepsakes.

2. Specialty Boutique

Location: Near the café on the fifth floor.

What You'll Find:

Limited Edition Items: Products tied to current temporary exhibitions.

Children's Section: Art-themed games, puzzles, and coloring books.

Home Decor: Artistic items like mugs, scarves, and decorative objects inspired by the museum's collection.

Why Visit:

Unique and exclusive items not available in the main shop.

Great for collectors or those looking for one-of-a-kind finds.

Tips for Dining and Shopping at the Musée d'Orsay

1. Plan Your Timing:

The café and restaurant can get busy during peak hours (12–2 PM), so consider dining earlier or later for a quieter experience.

2. Combine Activities:

Stop by the café for a coffee break after visiting the upper floors, then head to the gift shop on your way out.

3. Budget Wisely:

While the dining options and gift shops are excellent, they can be pricey. Decide ahead of time what you'd like to splurge on.

4. Check for Exclusive Items:

Look for products tied to current exhibitions or seasonal specials, as these are often limited in availability.

5. Take Your Time:

The gift shops are an experience in themselves, offering a delightful blend of art, culture, and creativity. Don't rush through them!

Eiffel Tower Tour

The Story Behind the Eiffel Tower

The Eiffel Tower, an enduring symbol of Paris and one of the most recognizable landmarks in the world, has a rich and fascinating history. Its construction was met with controversy, but it has since become a global icon of art, architecture, and innovation.

HOW TO SCAN

1. Open the camera app on your phone.

2. Point the camera at the QR code.

3. Ensure the QR code is within the viewfinder.

4. Wait for the notification or link to appear.

5. Tap the notification or link.

6. Follow the link or access the content associated with the QR code.

Origins of the Eiffel Tower

The Eiffel Tower was designed by the French engineer Gustave Eiffel and built as the centerpiece of the 1889 Exposition Universelle (World's Fair) held in Paris. This event celebrated the 100th anniversary of the French Revolution and showcased France's industrial prowess.

The Design Competition: The French government organized a competition to create a monumental structure that would symbolize modern engineering. Eiffel's design, conceived by his company's senior engineers Maurice Koechlin and Émile Nouguier, was selected out of more than 100 entries.

The Vision: Eiffel envisioned a structure that was not only a marvel of engineering but also a work of art. It was initially referred to as the "300-meter tower", emphasizing its height.

Construction of the Eiffel Tower

Engineering Feats:
The tower's construction began in 1887 and was completed in just over two years, in March 1889—an astonishing feat for the time.

The structure is made of wrought iron, chosen for its strength and malleability.

Over 18,000 iron parts were meticulously crafted and assembled using 2.5 million rivets.

The base of the tower required massive foundations to support the weight of the structure. Each of the four legs rests on a concrete foundation buried deep into the ground.

Workforce:
A team of about 300 workers assembled the tower. Safety measures, such as guardrails and screens, were introduced to minimize accidents—a pioneering practice in the late 19th century.

Controversy and Criticism

When the Eiffel Tower was unveiled, it faced scathing criticism from prominent artists, writers, and intellectuals of the era.

The "Protest of the 300": A group of Parisians, including renowned figures like Guy de Maupassant and Charles Gounod, signed a petition decrying the tower as an "ugly" and "monstrous" addition to the Parisian skyline.

Temporary Structure:
The tower was originally intended to stand for only 20 years. After the fair, it was slated for demolition, but its value as a radio transmission tower and its growing popularity saved it.

The Eiffel Tower's Transformation

Despite early criticism, the Eiffel Tower quickly gained recognition as a masterpiece of engineering and design.

A Symbol of Modernity:
By the early 20th century, the tower was embraced as a symbol of progress, innovation, and France's leadership in the industrial age.

Radio and Communication:
In 1903, the tower was used for the first radio transmission, cementing its importance in communication technology. During World War I, it played a crucial role in intercepting enemy communications.

Cultural Icon:
Over the decades, the Eiffel Tower has appeared in countless films, literature, and artworks, further solidifying its place as a global cultural icon.

Architectural Details and Innovations

Height: The Eiffel Tower originally stood at 312 meters (1,024 feet) and was the tallest man-made structure in the world until New York's Chrysler Building surpassed it in 1930. Today, with antennas, it measures 330 meters (1,083 feet).

Design Features:

The open lattice design was chosen to minimize wind resistance.

The shape of the tower, with its broad base and narrow top, provides exceptional stability.

Illumination:
The Eiffel Tower's nightly illumination began in 1925 with a series of light bulbs. Today, it features 20,000 sparkling lights, creating its iconic nighttime glow.

Enduring Legacy

Today, the Eiffel Tower is visited by over 7 million people annually, making it one of the most visited monuments in the world.

It symbolizes the beauty of Paris and the innovation of its creators.

From hosting daring stunts to celebrating global events, the Eiffel Tower has transcended its original purpose and become a timeless icon.

The story of the Eiffel Tower is one of resilience, creativity, and the power of vision—an inspiration to generations of visitors who stand beneath its iron arches and gaze up at its awe-inspiring height.

How to Plan Your Visit

The Eiffel Tower is one of the most visited monuments in the world, so planning your trip in advance can save time, reduce stress, and ensure a memorable experience. Here's everything you need to know about tickets, timing, and accessibility.

Tickets

1. Ticket Options:

Standard Tickets:

Stairs Access: Tickets to climb the stairs to the second floor.

Lift Access: Tickets for elevator access to the second floor or the summit.

Priority Access Tickets: Skip-the-line options for those short on time.

Guided Tours: Tickets often include access and a guide for a more in-depth experience.

Combined Tickets: Some packages include boat tours on the Seine or other Paris attractions.

2. Where to Buy:

Official Eiffel Tower website: www.toureiffel.paris (recommended for the best prices).

Third-party platforms like GetYourGuide or Viator for guided experiences.

3. Ticket Pricing (as of recent updates):

Stairs to the second floor: ~€11 for adults.

Elevator to the summit: ~€28 for adults.

Discounts are available for children, students, and disabled visitors.

4. Book in Advance:

Tickets can sell out quickly, especially during peak travel seasons. Aim to book several weeks ahead for guaranteed access.

Best Times to Visit

1. Early Morning:

Arrive when it opens (~9:30 AM) to avoid long lines and enjoy a quieter experience.

The morning light offers great photography opportunities.

2. Late Evening:

The Eiffel Tower lights up after sunset, creating a magical ambiance.

The last entry is usually around 10:30 PM (check seasonal variations).

3. Off-Peak Days:

Weekdays are generally less crowded than weekends.

Avoid major holidays and school vacations if possible.

4. Seasonal Considerations:

Spring (April–June) and Fall (September–October) offer pleasant weather and smaller crowds.

Summers are busy but ideal for longer daylight hours.

Winters are quieter, but dress warmly as it can get chilly at the top.

Accessibility

The Eiffel Tower is accessible to most visitors, including those with mobility challenges.

1. Elevator Access:

Elevators are available to the second floor and summit, accommodating wheelchairs.

However, stair access is not suitable for visitors with limited mobility.

2. Facilities:

Accessible restrooms are located on the ground and second floors.

Wheelchair users can visit the first and second floors but not the summit due to elevator restrictions.

3. Special Considerations:

Priority access is often available for disabled visitors.

Staff are helpful and can assist if needed—notify them upon arrival.

4. Tips for Accessibility:

Book tickets online to secure your slot.

Consider visiting during off-peak times for easier navigation.

Views From the Top: What to Spot

The Eiffel Tower offers unparalleled panoramic views of Paris, and each level provides a unique perspective.

Second Floor (115 meters/377 feet)

Landmarks to Spot:

Seine River: Observe its elegant flow and bridges.

Champs de Mars: The lush park stretching toward École Militaire.

Trocadéro Gardens: Across the Seine, with fountains and sculptures.

Louvre Museum: To the northeast, its glass pyramid is visible.

Notre-Dame Cathedral: Look east for its Gothic spires.

Why It's Special:

This level offers the best balance between height and visibility, making it a favorite for photographers.

Summit (276 meters/906 feet)

Experience:

The highest publicly accessible point in Paris.

Feel the breeze and marvel at the sheer scale of the city below.

Landmarks to Spot:

Sacré-Cœur Basilica: Perched on Montmartre Hill.

La Défense: The modern skyline of Paris to the west.

Les Invalides: The golden dome is unmistakable.

Arc de Triomphe: At the western end of the Champs-Élysées.

Champagne Bar: Treat yourself to a glass of champagne at the summit for a luxurious experience.

Nighttime Views

The illuminated city transforms into the City of Light at night.

Spot twinkling landmarks like the Seine bridges and the glowing Champs-Élysées.

Don't miss the Eiffel Tower's own hourly light show—a dazzling spectacle visible from the summit.

By planning your visit carefully and knowing what to expect at each level, the Eiffel Tower experience becomes a highlight of your Paris adventure. From strategic ticket purchases to taking in the stunning views, every detail contributes to a memorable journey to the heart of Parisian charm.

Nearby Attractions and Photo Opportunities

The Eiffel Tower's central location makes it the perfect starting point for exploring iconic Parisian landmarks and discovering picturesque photo spots. Whether you're seeking historical sites, green spaces, or romantic views, the area surrounding the tower offers something for everyone.

Nearby Attractions

1. Champs de Mars

Distance: Directly beneath the Eiffel Tower.

What to See:

This sprawling park offers spectacular views of the tower, making it an ideal spot for a relaxing stroll or a picnic.

Look for the Wall for Peace, a modern art installation promoting global harmony.

Why Visit: It's a great spot for both daytime and evening photography, with the tower's sparkling lights as a backdrop.

2. Trocadéro Gardens

Distance: ~5-minute walk across the Seine.

What to See:

Famous for its Palais de Chaillot, housing museums like the Cité de l'Architecture et du Patrimoine.

Fountains of Trocadéro: These grand fountains create stunning reflections of the Eiffel Tower.

Why Visit: The elevated terraces provide one of the best panoramic views of the tower.

3. Musée du Quai Branly – Jacques Chirac

Distance: ~7-minute walk.

What to See:

A museum dedicated to the indigenous art and cultures of Africa, Asia, Oceania, and the Americas.

Its lush garden and unique architecture are worth exploring.

Why Visit: A cultural escape that complements your Eiffel Tower experience.

4. Pont de Bir-Hakeim

Distance: ~10-minute walk.

What to See:

This elegant double-decked bridge is famous for its symmetrical arches and cinematic charm (featured in films like Inception).

Why Visit: A lesser-crowded location offering dramatic views of the tower and the Seine.

5. École Militaire

Distance: ~15-minute walk through Champs de Mars.

What to See:

This grand military school has an impressive facade and historical significance as Napoleon Bonaparte's alma mater.

Why Visit: Combine history with a unique perspective of the Eiffel Tower behind the building.

Photo Opportunities

1. Classic Full-Tower Shots

Location: Champs de Mars or Trocadéro Gardens.

Why It Works: These open spaces provide unobstructed views of the Eiffel Tower, ideal for capturing its full height and symmetry.

2. Reflection Photos

Location: Trocadéro Fountains.

Tip: Arrive early to avoid crowds and photograph the tower's reflection in the water for a serene effect.

3. Artistic Framing

Location: Pont de Bir-Hakeim.

Why It Works: Use the bridge's iron framework to naturally frame the Eiffel Tower in your shot.

4. Up-Close Perspectives

Location: Beneath the Eiffel Tower.

Why It Works: Experiment with wide-angle lenses to emphasize the intricate iron latticework.

5. Romantic Views

Location: Seine River Cruises.

Why It Works: Capture the tower from a unique, dynamic angle as you float past it on the water.

6. Nighttime Glow

Location: Trocadéro Gardens or Pont Alexandre III.

Why It Works: The Eiffel Tower's hourly light show offers a dazzling photo opportunity. Use a tripod for long-exposure shots to highlight the sparkling lights.

7. Seasonal Highlights

Spring: Cherry blossoms in Champs de Mars add a pop of color to your photos.

Winter: The tower often glows through a misty Parisian evening, creating a magical ambiance.

Tips for the Best Photos

Golden Hour: Visit during sunrise or sunset for softer lighting and fewer crowds.

Night Photography: Use a tripod for stability and capture the glowing lights with a long exposure.

Explore Angles: Walk around the base, the Seine, and surrounding streets to find unexpected perspectives.

Consider the Weather: Cloudy skies can add drama, while sunny days create crisp, vibrant shots.

By pairing your Eiffel Tower visit with nearby attractions and carefully chosen photo spots, you'll leave with not just unforgettable memories but also frame-worthy images of your time in Paris.

Rue Cler Walk

A Guide to Parisian Street Markets

Rue Cler, nestled in the heart of Paris's 7th arrondissement, is a quintessential Parisian market street offering a glimpse into local life. Known for its charming cobblestone path, vibrant storefronts, and friendly atmosphere, it's the perfect destination for food lovers, photographers, and anyone looking to experience Paris like a local.

What Makes Rue Cler Special?

Authentic Parisian Atmosphere

Rue Cler is less touristy than other parts of Paris, allowing visitors to experience the city's everyday rhythm. Locals frequent the street for their daily shopping, fostering an inviting and relaxed environment.

Gourmet Paradise

The street is lined with specialty food shops, including fromageries, patisseries, charcuteries, and épiceries. It's a treasure trove for those looking to sample the best of French gastronomy.

Accessible and Walkable

Rue Cler's pedestrian-friendly layout makes it easy to explore on foot. The compact size ensures you can leisurely browse without feeling overwhelmed.

Highlights of Rue Cler

Fresh Produce Stalls

Vibrant displays of seasonal fruits and vegetables are the first things to catch your eye.

Vendors are known for their high-quality goods, often sourced from regional farms.

Artisan Shops

Cheese Shops (Fromageries): Try classics like Camembert, Brie, and Comté. Don't hesitate to ask the cheesemonger for recommendations.

Bakeries (Boulangeries): Stop by a patisserie for buttery croissants, pain au chocolat, or a freshly baked baguette.

Wine and Spirits

Specialty wine shops offer a curated selection of French wines. You can also find Champagne, perfect for a celebratory picnic.

Meat and Charcuterie

Discover expertly crafted pâtés, sausages, and cured meats. Some shops offer ready-to-eat options for on-the-go enjoyment.

Florists and Cafés

Colorful flower stands add to Rue Cler's charm. Nearby cafés provide the ideal spot for people-watching with a café crème or glass of wine.

How to Experience Rue Cler Like a Local

1. Arrive Early

Visit in the morning to see the market at its liveliest. Vendors are more engaged, and the selection is at its freshest.

2. Shop for a Picnic

Pick up a mix of cheese, charcuterie, bread, and wine to enjoy at nearby Champs de Mars, with the Eiffel Tower as your backdrop.

3. Talk to the Vendors

Parisians are passionate about their products. Strike up a conversation to learn about their specialties. A little French goes a long way!

4. Blend in

Carry a reusable shopping bag and avoid oversized cameras. Dressing neatly helps you blend into the crowd and enhances your local experience.

Practical Information

Location

Rue Cler is located in the 7th arrondissement, near the Eiffel Tower and École Militaire.

Hours of Operation

Shops typically open between 8:00 AM and 7:30 PM.

Markets are busiest in the morning, and many establishments close on Mondays and during lunchtime.

Getting There

Metro: Take Line 8 to École Militaire station, just a short walk from Rue Cler.

Bus: Several bus routes stop nearby, including lines 80 and 92.

Tips for Exploring Rue Cler

1. Bring Cash: Some vendors may not accept credit cards.

2. Try Before You Buy: Many vendors offer samples, especially for cheese and charcuterie.

3. Pack Light: If you're planning to shop, leave extra space in your bag for goodies.

4. Be Patient: Weekends can be crowded, but the lively atmosphere is worth it.

Rue Cler in a Nutshell

Rue Cler is more than just a market street; it's a celebration of Parisian culture, gastronomy, and community. Whether you're assembling a gourmet picnic, sampling French delicacies, or simply soaking in the ambiance, this charming street offers a unique and memorable Parisian experience.

Sampling Fresh Produce, Cheese, and Pastries

Rue Cler is a haven for food lovers, offering a sensory experience that showcases the best of French gastronomy. Strolling along this cobblestone market street, you'll encounter vibrant produce, rich cheeses, and buttery pastries that invite you to indulge.

Fresh Produce

Seasonal Variety: The stalls on Rue Cler brim with fresh fruits and vegetables, often locally sourced. From ripe summer strawberries to winter citrus, the selection reflects the changing seasons.

Tasting Tip: Vendors often allow you to sample their offerings. Try a slice of juicy melon or a handful of plump cherries for a quick refreshment.

What to Buy:

Summer: Apricots, peaches, and heirloom tomatoes.

Winter: Clementines, persimmons, and root vegetables.

Cheese

Fromageries to Explore:

Stop by La Fromagerie Cler for a curated selection of France's most iconic cheeses. The aroma alone is worth the visit!

Must-Try Cheeses:

Camembert: A creamy, mild favorite.

Roquefort: Perfect for blue cheese enthusiasts.

Comté: A nutty, aged cheese ideal for snacking or pairing with wine.

Tasting Tip: Ask the cheesemonger for pairing suggestions. Many shops will vacuum-seal your purchases for travel if you plan to bring cheese home.

Pastries

Bakeries to Visit:

Le Moulin de la Vierge: A charming boulangerie with an excellent selection of freshly baked bread and pastries.

Must-Try Treats:

Croissants: Flaky, buttery, and quintessentially French.

Pain au Chocolat: A chocolate-filled delight.

Éclairs: Filled with creamy custard and topped with a glossy glaze.

Tasting Tip: Buy a few items to sample as you stroll, or enjoy them with coffee at a nearby café.

Local Boutiques and Cafés

Rue Cler is not just about food—it's also home to boutique shops and cozy cafés that embody Parisian charm.

Local Boutiques

1. Flower Shops

Stalls overflowing with fresh blooms add bursts of color to Rue Cler. They're perfect for a gift or brightening your day.

2. Wine and Spirits

Visit Nicolas, a well-known wine shop, to pick up a bottle of French wine or Champagne. The staff is happy to recommend pairings for your cheese and charcuterie.

3. Specialty Stores

Shops selling olive oil, honey, and artisanal chocolates are scattered along the street, offering unique souvenirs and culinary treasures.

Cafés

1. Café du Marché

A popular spot with both locals and visitors, offering traditional French dishes and outdoor seating.

What to Try: Order a café crème and watch the world go by.

2. Les Deux Abeilles

A cozy tea room serving homemade quiches, tarts, and salads.

Why Visit: Its quaint ambiance is perfect for a quiet retreat after exploring the market.

Tips for Exploring Rue Cler's Boutiques and Cafés

Take Your Time: Boutique owners and café staff often enjoy chatting about their offerings. Don't rush your experience.

Seating Choices: Choose outdoor seating at cafés for a quintessential Parisian vibe, especially on sunny days.

Small Purchases: Many shops sell items in smaller quantities, ideal for sampling a variety of goods.

Make the Most of Your Visit

Combine fresh market finds with a leisurely café stop to experience Rue Cler's charm. Whether you're savoring artisanal cheese, picking up a bouquet of flowers, or enjoying a glass of wine, the street's vibrant energy and local flavor will leave a lasting impression.

Perfect Picnic Spots Near Rue Cler

Rue Cler's vibrant market scene makes it the perfect place to gather provisions for a quintessential Parisian picnic. Once you've picked up some fresh produce, artisanal cheese, charcuterie, and pastries, head to one of these idyllic spots nearby to enjoy your feast.

1. Champ de Mars

Located just a 10-minute walk from Rue Cler, the Champ de Mars is an expansive park offering unparalleled views of the Eiffel Tower.

Why It's Perfect:

Iconic View: The Eiffel Tower provides a breathtaking backdrop for your picnic.

Family-Friendly: Open spaces for children to play and benches for relaxing.

Accessibility: Easily reachable by foot or a short metro ride.

Tips:

Arrive early to secure a shaded spot under the trees.

Bring a blanket to sit comfortably on the grass.

Stay for the evening light show on the Eiffel Tower (every hour after sunset).

2. Esplanade des Invalides

Just a short walk from Rue Cler, this open area near Les Invalides is ideal for those seeking a quieter, less touristy picnic spot.

Why It's Perfect:

Historical Surroundings: Enjoy views of the magnificent Hôtel des Invalides, which houses Napoleon's tomb.

Spacious Grounds: Plenty of room to spread out, even on busy days.

Tips:

Pack lightweight picnic gear as the esplanade has fewer benches.

Stop by one of Rue Cler's wine shops for a bottle of French wine to accompany your meal.

3. Parc du Champ de l'Alma

This small, serene park is tucked away near the Seine and the Pont de l'Alma, offering a peaceful retreat.

Why It's Perfect:

River Views: Enjoy your meal while watching boats cruise along the Seine.

Intimate Setting: Smaller crowds make for a more relaxed atmosphere.

Tips:

Keep an eye on the time, as the park may have restricted hours in the evening.

Bring pastries from Rue Cler to enjoy as dessert after your main meal.

4. Trocadéro Gardens

For a panoramic view of the Eiffel Tower from a different angle, head to the Trocadéro Gardens, located across the Seine from Rue Cler.

Why It's Perfect:

Iconic Photo Ops: Capture postcard-worthy photos of the Eiffel Tower with your picnic setup.

Stunning Fountains: The gardens' fountains add to the picturesque ambiance.

Tips:

Arrive early to beat the crowds, especially during peak tourist seasons.

Combine your picnic with a stroll around the gardens to take in the sculptures and landscape.

5. Jardin des Tuileries

For a classic Parisian park experience, take a short metro ride or leisurely walk to the Jardin des Tuileries, near the Louvre.

Why It's Perfect:

Central Location: Close to major attractions, making it a convenient stop.

Elegant Ambiance: Beautifully manicured gardens, fountains, and statues surround you.

Tips:

Seating is available on green metal chairs scattered around the park.

Enjoy pastries from Rue Cler while relaxing by one of the fountains.

Essentials for a Parisian Picnic

1. Food: Grab baguettes, cheese, charcuterie, fresh fruits, and pastries from Rue Cler's shops.

2. Drink: Don't forget a bottle of wine or sparkling water. Many shops on Rue Cler offer picnic-ready beverages.

3. Blanket: Bring a lightweight blanket for grassy areas.

4. Utensils: Pack reusable utensils, napkins, and a corkscrew if you plan to open wine.

5. Trash Bag: Keep the area clean by collecting your trash before leaving.

Make Your Picnic Unforgettable

A Rue Cler picnic is more than just a meal—it's an immersion into Parisian life. Whether you choose the sprawling lawns of the Champ de Mars or the tranquil banks of the Seine, savor each bite and the surrounding beauty. Your perfect picnic will be a highlight of your Paris adventure!

Versailles Tour

The Palace - Must-See Rooms and Artwork

A trip to the Palace of Versailles is a journey into the grandeur of French history, art, and culture. Located just outside Paris, this opulent palace was once the home of French royalty, particularly during the reign of Louis XIV, known as the Sun King. The palace, its gardens, and the surrounding grounds form one of the most visited historical sites in the world. Here's a guide to the must-see rooms and iconic artwork within the palace to ensure you make the most of your visit.

1. The Hall of Mirrors (Galerie des Glaces)

The Hall of Mirrors is the crown jewel of the Palace of Versailles. This grand corridor, measuring 73 meters in length, is adorned with 357 mirrors that reflect the light from the grand windows that look out over the gardens.

Why It's a Must-See:

Historical Significance: It was here that the Treaty of Versailles was signed in 1919, ending World War I.

Architectural Splendor: The room is lined with majestic chandeliers, gilded moldings, and portraits of French monarchs. The mirrors were once a symbol of France's wealth and power.

Art and Decoration:

The ceiling paintings depict major events in the reign of Louis XIV. Highlights include "The Glory of Louis XIV", which portrays him as the Sun King, shining down upon his empire.

2. The King's Grand Apartments

The King's Apartments are a series of interconnected rooms that give you insight into the daily life of Louis XIV, as well as his sense of luxury and power. Each room is intricately designed and named after mythological figures, demonstrating the king's desire to link himself to divine power.

Must-See Rooms:

The King's Bedchamber: This was the central room of the King's Apartments and the setting for royal ceremonies, including the king's rising and retiring. The bed, although no longer present, remains a symbolic center of power.

The Salon of War: One of the most impressive rooms, decorated with paintings celebrating France's military victories.

The Salon of Peace: In contrast, this room is dedicated to peace and prosperity, with lavish artwork showing the peaceful reign of Louis XIV.

Art and Decoration:

The ceilings here are adorned with allegorical paintings celebrating the triumphs of the king and his reign. These include "The Triumph of Louis XIV" by Charles de la Fosse, celebrating his military victories.

3. The Queen's Grand Apartments

The Queen's Apartments were the private living quarters of the queen consort, and they showcase a slightly different aesthetic compared to the King's rooms. The apartments are more intimate but still richly decorated, offering a glimpse into the royal women's lives.

Must-See Rooms:

The Queen's Bedchamber: A beautiful, more serene counterpart to the King's Bedchamber, featuring intricate tapestries and a rococo-style design.

The Salon of Mercury: A stunning room adorned with fine furniture, chandeliers, and a portrait of Marie Antoinette.

The Salon of Venus: This room is dedicated to the queen's beauty and romanticized depictions of femininity.

Art and Decoration:

The Salon of Venus features mythological scenes of Venus, the goddess of love, surrounded by gilded decorations and mirrors.

4. The Chapel of Versailles (Chapelle Royale)

The Chapelle Royale is a stunning space used for religious services by the royal family. It is one of the most remarkable parts of Versailles, built in the Baroque style.

Why It's a Must-See:

Majestic Architecture: The chapel features a soaring vaulted ceiling, intricate stained-glass windows, and beautifully crafted marble floors.

Historical Importance: It was in this chapel that kings and queens were crowned and celebrated their religious ceremonies.

Art and Decoration:

The ceiling is painted with the "Glory of the Holy Trinity", emphasizing the divine right of kings, a crucial part of the French monarchy's legitimacy.

The chapel is also home to magnificent organ pipes, with performances occasionally taking place during visits.

5. The Royal Opera of Versailles

The Royal Opera House is an opulent space used for performances during the reign of Louis XV. This room showcases the artistic side of the monarchy, and is one of the most splendid rooms in the palace.

Why It's a Must-See:

Unique Design: It is one of the most beautiful opera houses in the world, with its rococo-style décor, gold-leaf detailing, and rich red velvet seats.

Music History: Performances were once given in this space for the royal court, including operas by composers like Jean-Baptiste Lully.

Art and Decoration:

The ceiling of the opera house is painted with scenes depicting the Greek gods, celebrating the cultural aspirations of the French monarchy.

6. The Gardens of Versailles

Though not part of the palace's interior, the Gardens of Versailles are an essential part of any visit to Versailles. Designed by André Le Nôtre, the gardens are a masterpiece of landscape architecture, blending nature and human design in an extraordinary way.

Why It's a Must-See:

The gardens cover over 800 hectares, offering fountains, statues, and perfectly manicured paths.

Fountains: The Latona Fountain and Apollo Fountain are particularly famous, each depicting mythological stories.

Tips:

Plan to spend a few hours walking through the gardens. The Grand Trianon and Petit Trianon on the grounds are also worth visiting.

Art and Collections

Versailles is not only an architectural marvel but also a repository of incredible artwork. While touring the palace, look out for the following:

Portraits of the Monarchs: Portraits of Louis XIV, Louis XV, and Louis XVI are scattered throughout the palace, highlighting their reigns and influence.

French Mythology in Art: The artwork throughout the palace often includes references to classical mythology, symbolizing the monarchy's divine right and power.

Tips for Touring the Palace of Versailles

1. Arrive Early: Versailles can get crowded, especially during peak tourist seasons. Arriving early will give you a chance to explore the palace at a more leisurely pace.

2. Consider a Guided Tour: To gain a deeper understanding of the historical context, a guided tour is highly recommended.

3. Wear Comfortable Shoes: The palace and gardens are vast, so wear comfortable shoes for walking.

4. Visit the Gardens: Don't miss out on exploring the vast, beautiful gardens.

Gardens and Fountains Tour

Gardens and Fountains Tour at Versailles

The Gardens of Versailles are one of the most iconic features of the Palace of Versailles, showcasing the grandeur and meticulous planning that epitomized French royalty during the reign of Louis XIV, also known as the Sun King. Designed by the famous landscape architect André Le Nôtre, the gardens stretch over 800 hectares and boast over 50 fountains, dozens of statues, and perfectly manicured lawns. Exploring these gardens offers a glimpse into the royal opulence and natural beauty that defined the period.

1. The Layout and Design of the Gardens

The layout of the gardens is based on the classical French style, with geometric patterns, symmetrical paths, and large expanses of lawn. The grand perspective of the garden is designed to draw the eye down long, straight avenues and lead to magnificent fountains and sculptures. The gardens are split into several distinct sections, including the Parterre du Midi, the Parterre d'Eau, and the Grand Canal, all contributing to the grandeur of the setting.

The Parterre du Midi, located near the main palace, features perfectly trimmed boxwood hedges, flowerbeds filled with vibrant seasonal blooms, and intricate patterns. It leads to the Parterre d'Eau, which is framed by large pools and small canals. These tranquil water features not only enhance the beauty of the landscape but also create a sense of harmony and tranquility in the midst of the royal estate.

2. The Fountains: A Water Spectacle

The fountains in the Gardens of Versailles are legendary, known for their sheer size and engineering marvel. The fountains were a feat of hydraulic engineering during the 17th century, powered by an elaborate system of pumps and water channels that channeled water from the Seine River to the palace. Some of the most famous fountains include:

The Fountain of Latona: Situated in the Grand Canal area, the Fountain of Latona is a large, dramatic sculpture representing the mythological goddess Latona and her children, Apollo and Diana. The fountain is surrounded by a series of cascading water features and symbolic sculptures.

The Fountain of Apollo: Located at the entrance to the Grand Canal, this fountain features a sculpture of the god Apollo rising from a chariot, surrounded by water jets and symbolic figures that represent the sun, reflecting Louis XIV's persona as the Sun King.

The Neptune Fountain: This is one of the largest and most spectacular fountains in the gardens, symbolizing the power of the sea. The fountain features Neptune, the god of the sea, surrounded by a series of impressive sculptures and water jets, creating a dramatic display of water.

3. The Musical Fountain Show

For an even more immersive experience, visitors can attend the Grandes Eaux or Musical Fountain Show, which takes place during the warmer months. The show incorporates classical music that plays in harmony with the fountains, creating a dynamic and magical atmosphere. The gardens are transformed into a stage where the water jets dance to the rhythm of the music, providing a memorable and sensory experience.

The fountain shows are a highlight of the Versailles Gardens, as they blend art, music, and nature into one grand spectacle. Check the Versailles schedule to ensure you catch this extraordinary display while visiting.

4. The Orangerie

At the end of the Grand Canal, the Orangerie of Versailles is home to an impressive collection of citrus trees and tropical plants. The Orangerie was built to house the palace's collection of fruit trees, which were brought inside during the winter months to protect them from the cold. Today, it stands as a beautiful example of French garden architecture and is home to some remarkable sculptures and works of art.

The Gardens of Versailles are an essential part of any visit to the Palace of Versailles, offering an expansive display of classical French landscape architecture. One of the most enchanting sections of the gardens is the Hamlet of Marie Antoinette, a charming retreat built for the queen in the late 18th century. This peaceful, pastoral area was a place where Marie Antoinette could escape the rigid formalities of court life and immerse herself in the more rustic aspects of country living.

The Hamlet of Marie Antoinette: A Refuge of Simplicity

Marie Antoinette, the last queen of France before the revolution, sought solace away from the opulence and political intrigue of the royal court. In 1783, she commissioned the creation of a small village within the Versailles estate, designed to mimic the rural French countryside. This Hamlet of Marie Antoinette, or Hameau de la Reine, was a reflection of her desire for a simpler life, although it was anything but simple in its construction and execution.

Why It's a Must-See:

A Place of Escape: The Hamlet served as a secluded getaway for Marie Antoinette, allowing her to experience a simpler, more rustic life, far removed from the formalities of Versailles. She would spend time in the hamlet with her closest friends, and occasionally, her children.

Historical Symbolism: The hamlet was part of a larger trend of romanticizing the pastoral life during the 18th century. The queen was attempting to break free from the rigid protocols of court life and reconnect with nature, albeit in a highly stylized form.

The Layout of the Hamlet

The Hamlet is designed as a miniature village, with idyllic cottages, a farm, and a picturesque lake, all set against the backdrop of the grand Versailles estate. The design of the Hamlet was created by the architect Richard Mique, and the construction was overseen by the queen herself. Although it was an area for leisure and play, its construction was a costly venture, further fueling public discontent with the queen's extravagant tastes.

Must-See Features:

The Queen's Dairy: One of the most iconic buildings in the Hamlet is the Queen's Dairy, a charming little structure designed to look like a rustic dairy farm. Inside, you can imagine Marie Antoinette and her companions engaging in pastoral activities like milking cows or churning butter. The architecture reflects the queen's desire to immerse herself in a rural lifestyle, yet it was a far cry from the modesty of actual country life.

The Farm: The farm at the Hamlet was equipped with various animals, including goats, cows, and poultry. It was also home to a small vegetable garden that provided the queen with fresh produce. While this farm was more about providing an idealized rural experience rather than a practical source of food, it added to the authenticity of the village setting.

The Boudoir of the Queen: Marie Antoinette's private boudoir in the Hamlet was another charming space designed to give her the feeling of living a simpler, more intimate life. This small, secluded room offers a glimpse into her personal escape from the royal court's rigid decorum. It's a quiet place to reflect on her life away from Versailles.

The Rustic Cottages: Each of the cottages in the Hamlet was designed with a different purpose in mind. Some were built for relaxation, others were meant for entertaining, and a few were even designed to look like traditional peasant homes. These cottages are a fascinating contrast to the grandeur of Versailles and offer insight into the queen's desire for a more modest and private lifestyle.

The Artificial Lake: At the heart of the Hamlet is a serene artificial lake, surrounded by trees and wildflowers. The lake was designed to evoke the feeling of the countryside and served as a peaceful retreat for the queen and her guests. The lake is still a tranquil area to explore, providing a quiet place to reflect on the royal history of Versailles.

Historical Significance and Symbolism

The Hamlet of Marie Antoinette is not just a retreat for leisure but a significant symbol of the disconnect between the monarchy and the French people during the years leading up to the Revolution. While the queen enjoyed the comforts of a rural life in the midst of extravagance, the common people were struggling in poverty. This lavish escape came to symbolize the monarchy's disconnect from the realities of the French populace, and its construction only served to deepen the resentment that would eventually contribute to the French Revolution.

The Queen's Image:

Marie Antoinette's spending habits and indulgence in lavish projects like the Hamlet were criticized by revolutionaries, who saw her as a symbol of aristocratic excess. The queen's desire to surround herself with rustic simplicity in a palace of grandeur was seen as an extravagant display of excess, which played a role in her eventual downfall.

Exploring the Hamlet Today

Today, the Hamlet of Marie Antoinette is a peaceful corner of the Versailles estate, offering visitors a chance to experience an entirely different side of the palace grounds. The rustic cottages, winding paths, and serene lake create a sense of escape from the hustle and bustle of the more crowded parts of the palace.

Things to Do:

Stroll the Grounds: Take your time exploring the grounds, walking through the quaint cottages, and marveling at the beautiful gardens and wildflowers. The area is far less crowded than the main palace, offering a quiet and reflective atmosphere.

Photography: The natural beauty of the Hamlet, combined with its historical significance, makes it a perfect spot for photography. The cottages and surrounding greenery make for picturesque photos, especially during the golden hours of morning or late afternoon.

Learn About the History: Take time to learn about the significance of the Hamlet and how it reflects the life of Marie Antoinette. The contrast between the rural fantasy and the political reality of the time adds depth to the experience.

Nearby Attractions

While visiting the Hamlet, you are already on the grounds of the Palace of Versailles, so don't miss the opportunity to explore other nearby attractions:

The Gardens of Versailles: The French formal gardens, designed by André Le Nôtre, are an absolute must-see. The vast, meticulously manicured lawns, fountains, and sculptures are iconic.

The Grand Trianon: A smaller palace located within the Versailles estate, the Grand Trianon was used as a retreat by the French kings and queens, including Louis XIV and Louis XV. The palace is renowned for its elegant architecture and tranquil gardens.

Tips for Visiting the Hamlet

1. Visit in the Morning or Late Afternoon: The Hamlet is often quieter in the early morning or late afternoon, allowing you to experience it in a more peaceful atmosphere.

2. Wear Comfortable Shoes: The area involves walking through gardens and unpaved paths, so comfortable footwear is essential.

3. Combine with a Visit to the Gardens: The Hamlet is located within the Versailles Gardens, so it's easy to combine both experiences on your visit.

Tips for Avoiding Crowds at Versailles

The Palace of Versailles is one of the most visited attractions in France, attracting millions of visitors each year. To fully enjoy the beauty and history of Versailles without the crowds, here are some practical tips to help you plan your visit:

1. Visit During the Off-Peak Seasons

The timing of your visit plays a significant role in how crowded Versailles will be. The busiest months tend to be in the summer, particularly July and August, when tourists flock to Paris.

Off-Peak Seasons:

Spring (March to May) and Autumn (September to November) are ideal times to visit. The weather is pleasant, and there are fewer tourists compared to the summer.

Winter months (December to February) are also a good option, especially if you don't mind cooler weather. While the gardens may not be in full bloom, the palace is less crowded, allowing you to explore more freely.

2. Arrive Early or Late in the Day

To avoid the busiest crowds, plan to arrive either early in the morning or later in the afternoon.

Early Morning: Arrive before the gates open (typically around 9:00 AM) to enjoy the palace before the tour buses and large groups arrive. The first hour of your visit will be quieter, allowing you to explore the main rooms of the palace, including the Hall of Mirrors, in peace.

Late Afternoon: If you can't make it first thing in the morning, aim to visit the palace later in the day, preferably after 3:00 PM. Most tourists will have left by then, especially those on day trips. The gardens and some sections of the palace stay open later, giving you a more relaxed experience.

3. Avoid Weekends

Weekends, particularly Saturdays and Sundays, tend to be much busier as both locals and tourists visit Versailles. To avoid the heavy crowds:

Weekdays (Monday to Friday) are the best days for a quieter experience. If possible, aim for a visit midweek when fewer visitors come.

4. Book Skip-the-Line Tickets

One of the best ways to avoid waiting in long lines is to book skip-the-line tickets in advance. These tickets will give you access to a faster entry point, allowing you to bypass the typically long queues at the entrance. Some skip-the-line options also include guided tours, which offer insightful commentary while allowing you to skip the main crowds.

Online Booking: Purchase your tickets in advance via the official Versailles website or a trusted tour operator to avoid wasting time in line.

5. Explore the Gardens Early or Late

The Gardens of Versailles are one of the most popular parts of the estate, but you can avoid the crowds by timing your visit carefully.

Morning: Arriving early, especially when the gardens first open, is a good way to experience the fountains and flowerbeds before the midday crowds arrive.

Evening: The gardens are still open after the palace closes, giving you a peaceful and scenic experience as the sun begins to set. The evening light offers beautiful photo opportunities, and the crowds thin out significantly.

6. Visit the Trianon Palaces and the Hamlet

While the main palace is typically crowded, the Grand Trianon and Petit Trianon, as well as the Hamlet of Marie Antoinette, are often less crowded, especially later in the day. These areas offer a more serene atmosphere and are less likely to be filled with large tourist groups.

Petit Trianon and Grand Trianon: These smaller palaces offer insight into the private lives of the royals. They are tucked away from the main palace and are often much quieter, providing a more intimate experience.

7. Use Audio Guides or Apps to Avoid Group Tours

Large groups can create a bustling atmosphere and block your path as they move from room to room. If you want to avoid these groups, consider using an audio guide or a mobile app with a self-guided tour. This allows you to explore at your own pace, avoiding crowds while still learning about the palace's rich history.

8. Time Your Visit with Special Events

Versailles hosts special events, such as musical fountain shows or nighttime illuminations. These events can draw larger crowds to certain areas, so if you're looking to avoid them, check the event schedule before you go. If you're interested in seeing these unique displays, arriving early will help you beat the crowds.

9. Be Strategic in Your Path

When you enter the palace, follow a less common path to avoid the large groups that typically visit the most popular areas (e.g., Hall of Mirrors). After you explore some of the less crowded rooms and wings, you can then visit the more popular rooms when they are less busy, typically later in the morning or in the afternoon.

10. Be Prepared to Walk

The Palace of Versailles and its expansive grounds require a fair amount of walking. To make the most of your visit, prepare for a full day of exploring. This includes walking through the gardens, visiting the Trianon Palaces, and taking in the beautiful landscapes. If you're physically prepared for a day of walking, you'll feel less pressured by the crowds and be able to appreciate the beauty of Versailles without rushing.

11. Check for Museum Closures or Renovations

Occasionally, certain parts of the palace or gardens may be closed for renovations or restoration work, which can limit your access to certain areas but may also result in fewer crowds. It's always worth checking the Versailles website or tourist information for any notices on closures before your visit.

Sights

Montmartre and the Sacré-Cœur: A Charming and Historic Parisian Gem

Montmartre, one of Paris's most beloved districts, offers a unique blend of history, art, and panoramic views of the city. Perched atop a hill in the 18th arrondissement, Montmartre was once the artistic heart of Paris, drawing painters, writers, and intellectuals throughout the 19th and early 20th centuries. Today, it retains a bohemian charm, making it a must-visit for anyone seeking to experience the city's artistic legacy and breathtaking views.

1. The Sacré-Cœur Basilica: A Majestic Landmark

At the summit of Montmartre sits the Sacré-Cœur Basilica, one of Paris's most iconic landmarks. With its gleaming white exterior, the basilica dominates the skyline of the city and offers some of the best panoramic views in Paris.

History and Architecture

The Sacré-Cœur was built in the late 19th century as a symbol of national hope and spiritual renewal following France's defeat in the Franco-Prussian War of 1870. Designed by architect Paul Abadie, the basilica is a masterpiece of Romanesque-Byzantine architecture. Its striking white travertine stone exterior ensures it stands out against the Paris skyline.

The basilica is also known for its dome, which rises 83 meters above the ground. Visitors can climb up to the top for a spectacular view of Paris that stretches out all the way to the Eiffel Tower and beyond.

Inside the Basilica

Inside the basilica, visitors are greeted by an awe-inspiring interior. The massive mosaic of Christ in Majesty, located above the altar, is one of the largest mosaics in the world. The overall feeling inside the basilica is one of reverence and peace, with visitors often sitting in silence or participating in mass.

2. The Stunning Views From Montmartre

One of the most compelling reasons to visit Montmartre is its views of Paris. Standing at the base of the Sacré-Cœur, you'll be treated to breathtaking vistas that are simply unparalleled in the city. The vantage point offers a sweeping panorama of Paris's rooftops, with key landmarks like the Eiffel Tower, Louvre, Notre-Dame, and Arc de Triomphe visible in the distance.

For an even more spectacular experience, you can ascend to the dome of the basilica, which offers a 360-degree view. On clear days, you can see for miles, and it's an excellent spot for photography.

3. Exploring the Streets of Montmartre

Beyond the Sacré-Cœur, Montmartre's charm is in its narrow streets, historic cafés, and artistic heritage. Walking through the Place du Tertre, you'll find artists showcasing their paintings and portraits, much like they did during the times of Pablo Picasso and Vincent van Gogh, who both lived and worked in the area. The square retains much of its artistic atmosphere and is a favorite for tourists and locals alike.

Hidden Gems in Montmartre

Le Mur des Je T'aime: A tribute to love, this wall in the Jehan Rictus garden is covered with "I love you" written in over 250 languages. It's a perfect spot for a romantic moment or a unique photo.

La Maison Rose: A historic café that was once frequented by artists like Amedeo Modigliani and Maurice Utrillo, La Maison Rose is a picturesque spot offering classic French dishes and an inviting atmosphere.

The Montmartre Cemetery: A quieter and more somber part of Montmartre, this cemetery is home to the graves of famous artists and writers, including Dalida, Emile Zola, and Francis Poulenc. It's an off-the-beaten-path gem that offers a peaceful escape from the crowds.

4. The Artistic Legacy of Montmartre

Montmartre is perhaps best known for its rich artistic history. In the late 19th and early 20th centuries, this area was the home and studio for some of the world's most famous artists, including Henri Toulouse-Lautrec, Edgar Degas, Pablo Picasso, and Vincent van Gogh. The neighborhood's bohemian atmosphere, with its cafés, cabarets, and vibrant street life, inspired many of the great works of modern art.

Le Bateau-Lavoir: A famous artist's studio where Picasso lived and worked during the early years of his career. Though the building was destroyed by fire in the 1970s, the site still carries historical significance.

Musée de Montmartre: This museum is dedicated to the history of Montmartre's artistic past. Housed in a charming 17th-century building, it exhibits works by artists who were once residents, and the history of the neighborhood, including its role in the early development of impressionism.

5. Visiting Montmartre at Different Times of Day

Montmartre changes dramatically depending on the time of day. Here's how to enjoy the district at various times:

Morning: The area is peaceful in the early hours before the crowds arrive. You can enjoy the quiet beauty of the Sacré-Cœur and wander through the streets before the hustle and bustle of tourists fills the area. It's a great time for photography, with the soft morning light illuminating the picturesque streets.

Afternoon: As the day progresses, Montmartre becomes livelier, with visitors flooding the streets and cafés. This is the best time to stroll around the Place du Tertre, where you can watch artists at work or have your portrait drawn.

Evening: In the evening, Montmartre takes on a romantic atmosphere, with the lights of the city twinkling below. Many of the local bistros and cafés offer a perfect setting for dinner, where you can enjoy traditional French cuisine. The view of Paris from the Sacré-Cœur at sunset or after dark is nothing short of magical.

6. How to Get to Montmartre

Montmartre is well-connected to the rest of Paris by public transport.

By Metro: The Anvers (Line 2) and Pigalle (Lines 2 and 12) stations are both within walking distance of Montmartre. From there, you can take the Funicular to the top of the hill, or enjoy the walk up the Rue de Steinkerque.

Walking: For those who are up for a little exercise, you can walk up from the Abbesses Metro station through the winding streets of Montmartre, or take the famous Staircase of Montmartre, which provides a fantastic view of the city as you climb.

The Marais District: History and Modern Charm

The Marais is one of Paris's most vibrant and eclectic neighborhoods, blending historic architecture, trendy boutiques, and a rich cultural heritage. Nestled in the 3rd and 4th arrondissements, the Marais has undergone a remarkable transformation over the years. Once a medieval district that was home to the nobility, it now serves as a dynamic hub for fashion, food, and art, all while retaining its old-world charm.

A Historic Jewel of Paris

The Marais' history dates back to the 12th century when it was primarily marshland, hence its name. During the 16th century, it became the city's aristocratic quarter, with mansions and hôtels particuliers (private mansions) built by the rich and powerful. These buildings, many of which still stand today, are architectural masterpieces that reflect the grandeur of the era.

The district also played a central role in Paris's Jewish community, particularly in the Pletzl area, a thriving Jewish neighborhood since the 13th century. The Musée d'Art et d'Histoire du Judaïsme offers an intriguing look at the history and culture of Jews in France, making it an important stop for history buffs.

Trendy and Modern Vibes

Today, the Marais is a fusion of the old and new. The district's narrow, cobblestone streets are lined with chic boutiques, artisanal shops, and contemporary galleries. You can explore trendy cafes and enjoy the blend of historic and modern Parisian life. Le BHV Marais, a historic department store, is a great spot for shopping, offering a mix of classic Parisian goods alongside modern fashion and design.

A perfect day in the Marais could start with a visit to the Place des Vosges, one of the oldest and most beautiful squares in Paris, surrounded by arcades and elegant mansions. From there, you can wander through the charming streets, stopping at art galleries, cafes, and the famous Marché des Enfants Rouges, Paris's oldest covered market, where you can sample gourmet food from around the world.

Cultural and Artistic Epicenter

The Marais is home to many of Paris's top museums, including the Musée Picasso, which houses an extensive collection of the artist's work, and the Musée Carnavalet, dedicated to the history of Paris itself. Visitors can also explore Hôtel de Ville (City Hall), which hosts temporary art exhibitions and events.

The Marais: A Mix of Old and New

The Marais is a district that invites exploration. From its medieval roots to its contemporary offerings, the neighborhood is an embodiment of Paris's ability to embrace the old and the new. Whether you are admiring the historic architecture, shopping in the latest fashion boutiques, or enjoying an afternoon in one of its trendy cafés, the Marais never fails to charm.

Champs-Élysées and the Arc de Triomphe: Paris's Grand Avenue

The Champs-Élysées is undoubtedly one of the most famous avenues in the world, synonymous with luxury, elegance, and grandeur. Stretching for 1.9 kilometers from the Place de la Concorde to the Arc de Triomphe, it is a must-see destination for any visitor to Paris. Its wide tree-lined sidewalks, luxury boutiques, theaters, cafes, and monuments have made it a symbol of French sophistication and a central artery in the life of the city.

A Historical Avenue

The Champs-Élysées was once a swampy area before it was transformed into a grand avenue by Marie de Médicis in the 17th century. Its name, which means "Elysian Fields" in French, evokes the idea of paradise or eternal rest, and it certainly lives up to that idyllic imagery with its grand sweep of greenery and opulent surroundings.

In the 19th century, the avenue became even more prominent, hosting parades, celebrations, and national events. It was also the site of several historical moments, such as the Nazi occupation of Paris during WWII and the post-war liberation celebrations in 1944. Today, it still serves as the site for national events like the annual Bastille Day military parade.

The Arc de Triomphe: A Monumental Tribute

At the western end of the Champs-Élysées stands the majestic Arc de Triomphe, one of Paris's most famous landmarks. Commissioned by Napoleon Bonaparte after his victory at Austerlitz in 1805, the arch was designed to honor the French military and the soldiers who fought for France. Standing 50 meters tall, the arch is an impressive sight and serves as a reminder of France's rich and tumultuous history.

Visitors can climb the 284 steps to reach the top of the arch, where they are rewarded with a panoramic view of Paris. From here, you can spot the Eiffel Tower, the Louvre, and the sprawling boulevards that make up the city's famous landscape.

Luxury Shopping and Culture

The Champs-Élysées is often referred to as the "world's most beautiful avenue", and for good reason. Lined with luxurious stores like Louis Vuitton, Cartier, and Chanel, it's a shopper's paradise. The avenue also boasts iconic theaters like the Lido de Paris, where visitors can enjoy cabaret shows, as well as cinemas, cafés, and restaurants offering fine French cuisine.

For those seeking cultural enrichment, the Grand Palais and Petit Palais, both located along the avenue, are excellent places to explore. These museums host temporary exhibitions of world-class art and culture, from classic to contemporary works.

A Walk Down the Champs-Élysées

Walking down the Champs-Élysées is an experience in itself. The vibrant atmosphere, the stylish Parisians, the luxury boutiques, and the wide open space of the avenue combine to make this a quintessential Parisian experience. As you stroll, you can stop to enjoy the sights, indulge in a café au lait at one of the terrace cafés, or visit one of the avenue's many attractions.

The Avenue's Role in Modern Paris

Today, the Champs-Élysées is not only a historical and cultural landmark but also a lively hub for entertainment and commerce. It hosts some of the most popular events in Paris, including the annual Champs-Élysées Film Festival and the Tour de France finish line. As the avenue stretches toward the Place de la Concorde, it continues to serve as a focal point for celebrations, protests, and gatherings that reflect the pulse of Parisian life.

A Walk Through Time and Splendor

The Champs-Élysées and Arc de Triomphe are more than just tourist attractions—they represent the grandeur and beauty of Paris in a way few other places can. From the sweeping grandeur of the avenue to the monumental majesty of the arch, these iconic symbols of French culture and history offer a journey through time and modernity. Whether you are walking down the avenue, admiring the view from the Arc, or indulging in high-end shopping, the Champs-Élysées is a must-see for anyone visiting the City of Light.

Boat Rides on the Seine: A Scenic View of Paris from the Water

The Seine River winds its way through the heart of Paris, offering some of the most breathtaking and iconic views of the city. A boat ride along the Seine is a must-do activity, allowing visitors to experience Paris from a unique perspective, passing by historical landmarks, grand bridges, and picturesque riverbanks. Whether you're looking for a romantic evening cruise, a leisurely afternoon ride, or a cultural experience, the Seine offers a range of options to suit all tastes.

Types of Boat Rides

There are several different types of boat tours on the Seine, each offering its own experience of the city:

Sightseeing Cruises: These are the most popular and commonly available boat tours along the Seine. They often last between one and two hours and provide commentary about the landmarks you pass, such as the Eiffel Tower, Notre-Dame Cathedral, Louvre

Museum, Musée d'Orsay, and Pont Neuf. Many of these tours depart from the Port de la Bourdonnais, near the Eiffel Tower.

Dinner Cruises: For a more luxurious and romantic experience, consider a dinner cruise along the Seine. These cruises typically take place in the evening and offer a gourmet meal while you glide past illuminated landmarks. A dinner cruise allows you to savor Parisian cuisine while enjoying the romantic ambiance of the city by night.

Private Boat Rentals: If you prefer a more intimate and personalized experience, private boat rentals are available. You can rent small boats, such as a electric boat for a self-guided tour or a luxury yacht for a more lavish experience, perfect for special occasions like anniversaries or celebrations.

The Best Time for a Boat Ride

While the Seine is beautiful at any time of day, the views vary significantly depending on when you go. Daytime boat rides offer fantastic opportunities to see the landmarks bathed in natural light, while sunset and evening cruises provide a magical, twinkling view of the city with the lights reflecting off the water. Particularly, the Eiffel Tower's nightly light show, which sparkles every hour on the hour after sunset, is a highlight of evening cruises.

Where to Board

You can board boat tours at various points along the Seine. The most common departure points are near the Eiffel Tower (Port de la Bourdonnais), the Notre-Dame Cathedral (Port de la Tournelle), and near Concorde or Pont Neuf. Tickets for most boat rides can be purchased at the docks or online in advance.

A View of Parisian Landmarks

During the boat ride, you'll pass by some of the most iconic landmarks in Paris, giving you an entirely different perspective of the city. The Pont Neuf, the oldest bridge in Paris, Pont Alexandre III, with its ornate sculptures, and the Eiffel Tower, always stand out as key attractions visible from the water. The Notre-Dame Cathedral, Musée d'Orsay, and the Louvre are just a few more historic buildings you'll see along the way.

Parks and Gardens: Paris's Green Oases

Paris is a city of elegance, culture, and history, and its parks and gardens are no exception. From grand, formal gardens to peaceful green spaces where you can unwind, the city offers an array of outdoor havens perfect for relaxation or recreation. Whether you're strolling through beautifully manicured grounds, enjoying a picnic, or simply seeking some respite from the bustling streets, Paris's parks and gardens offer a variety of experiences.

Luxembourg Gardens (Jardin du Luxembourg)

The Luxembourg Gardens is one of Paris's most beloved green spaces, located in the 6th arrondissement near the Latin Quarter. It's a vast and beautifully landscaped garden that dates back to the 17th century when it was created by Marie de Médicis, the widow of King Henry IV.

What to See: The gardens feature a blend of formal French and English-style landscapes, with perfectly trimmed hedges, fountains, statues, and flower beds. The centerpiece of the gardens is the Luxembourg Palace, which now houses the French Senate. The Medici Fountain, a grand marble fountain with a neoclassical design, is another standout feature of the park.

Activities: Luxembourg Gardens is ideal for leisurely walks, picnics, or simply relaxing. Children will enjoy the playgrounds and the small pond where they can rent miniature sailboats. The Orangerie, an elegant glass pavilion, hosts seasonal exhibitions.

Cultural Events: Throughout the year, the Luxembourg Gardens hosts cultural events, including outdoor theater performances, concerts, and even art exhibitions. It's a fantastic spot for visitors looking to enjoy a little culture in a relaxing setting.

Tuileries Gardens (Jardin des Tuileries)

The Tuileries Gardens are perhaps one of the most famous parks in Paris. Located between the Louvre Museum and the Place de la Concorde, these beautifully landscaped gardens are a symbol of French elegance.

What to See: Designed in the 17th century by Catherine de Médicis, the gardens are arranged in a formal French style, with neat rows of trees, fountains, and statues. Notable attractions in the gardens include the Grand Bassin (large pool) and the

Orangerie (home to Monet's famous Water Lilies).

Activities: Visitors can enjoy a leisurely walk along the central axis of the gardens, relax on one of the many green chairs around the fountains, or visit the Musée de l'Orangerie, a museum that houses impressionist and post-impressionist masterpieces. In the summer, there are carnival rides and open-air cafes, making it a lively and fun spot to spend an afternoon.

Best For: Those looking to combine art, history, and nature in one experience. The Tuileries offer a seamless blend of Paris's historic landmarks and green space.

Bois de Boulogne

If you're seeking a larger, more natural green space, head to the Bois de Boulogne, a vast park located on the western edge of Paris. Covering more than 2,000 acres, this park is ideal for those who enjoy outdoor sports or simply want to escape the urban bustle.

What to See: The park is home to lakes, forests, and meadows, as well as attractions like the Bois de Boulogne Lake, where you can rent rowboats. There's also the Bagatelle Gardens, a smaller, more intimate garden within the park with beautiful rose gardens.

Activities: The Bois de Boulogne is perfect for cycling, jogging, or simply exploring the extensive walking trails. There are also several horseback riding stables and places for boating and picnics.

Best For: Nature lovers and those seeking an escape from the city's noise, or those with more active interests.

Parc des Buttes-Chaumont

In the 19th arrondissement, you'll find Parc des Buttes-Chaumont, a park known for its hilly terrain, dense trees, and impressive views. Unlike the more formal gardens of Paris, the Buttes-Chaumont has a natural, rugged feel, with cliffs, waterfalls, and a lake.

What to See: The park's most famous feature is its Temple of Sybil, a replica of an ancient Roman temple perched on a rocky hilltop. The park also has a suspension bridge, caves, and winding pathways that lead to secluded spots ideal for picnicking or relaxing.

Activities: The Buttes-Chaumont is great for a peaceful walk, photography, or simply escaping the hustle and bustle. There are also cafés and kiosks around the park where you can grab a snack or drink.

A Green Retreat in the Heart of Paris

Paris's parks and gardens offer visitors an opportunity to take a break from the busy streets and immerse themselves in nature, history, and beauty. Whether you prefer the formal elegance of the Luxembourg and Tuileries Gardens or the natural, tranquil atmosphere of the Bois de Boulogne or Buttes-Chaumont, there's a green oasis in Paris for everyone to enjoy. These parks and gardens are not only essential parts of the city's landscape but also cherished spaces for both locals and visitors to unwind and experience a more peaceful side of Paris.

Activities

Paris by Night: Cabarets and Cruises

When the night falls, Paris truly comes alive, offering a range of vibrant activities that capture the essence of its culture, entertainment, and romantic allure. Two of the most iconic ways to experience Paris by night are through cabarets and river cruises, each offering a distinct yet unforgettable experience that lets you see the city's beauty in a whole new light.

Cabarets: A Taste of Parisian Glamour

Paris's cabarets are legendary, offering a mix of dazzling performances, lavish costumes, and a vibrant atmosphere. These shows are a quintessential part of the city's cultural heritage and provide a lively glimpse into the French love for music, dance, and spectacle. Whether you're looking to experience the opulence of old-world Paris or enjoy a more modern twist on entertainment, Paris has something for everyone.

Moulin Rouge: The Iconic Cabaret

No list of Paris cabarets would be complete without mentioning the Moulin Rouge, the most famous cabaret in the world. Located in the heart of Montmartre, this iconic venue has been a symbol of Parisian nightlife since 1889. Known for its iconic French Cancan dance, the Moulin Rouge offers visitors a glamorous show full of high-energy dance routines, vibrant costumes, and mesmerizing choreography. The shows are often complemented by delicious dinner options, where you can enjoy classic French cuisine while watching the performances.

What to Expect: The performances at the Moulin Rouge are a dazzling mix of dance, music, and theatrics. Expect to see acrobatics, showgirls in sparkling costumes, and extravagant sets that transport you to another era. It's a true spectacle, ideal for those looking for a night of excitement and glamour.

Best For: Visitors who want to immerse themselves in a piece of Parisian history and experience the epitome of cabaret entertainment.

Le Lido: The Art of French Burlesque

Another iconic cabaret in Paris is Le Lido, located on the famous Champs-Élysées. Known for its sophisticated and artistic performances, Le Lido is more refined than the Moulin Rouge but no less spectacular. The shows here feature world-class dancers, elegant costumes, and lavish stage productions that often include water features and impressive lighting effects.

What to Expect: Le Lido's performances are centered around themes of elegance and beauty, with some shows even incorporating acrobatics and daring acts. The venue itself has a chic, glamorous atmosphere, making it perfect for a night out in Paris.

Best For: Those who prefer a more refined, sophisticated cabaret experience, with a focus on elegance and artistry.

Crazy Horse: A Contemporary Twist on Burlesque

For those seeking a more modern, edgy cabaret experience, Crazy Horse offers a contemporary take on the classic Parisian burlesque. Located near the Champs-Élysées, Crazy Horse is known for its seductive, avant-garde performances that celebrate femininity and sensuality. The venue prides itself on blending cutting-edge technology, minimalistic décor, and the art of striptease in a way that feels fresh and innovative.

What to Expect: Expect sleek, sensual performances with a focus on lighting, sound, and the art of seduction. The cabaret shows are visually stunning, and the minimalist, artistic approach makes this an intriguing alternative to more traditional cabaret experiences.

Best For: Visitors seeking a modern, high-concept cabaret with a focus on sensuality, art, and performance.

Seine River Cruises: A Romantic Tour of Paris

Another iconic Parisian experience that should not be missed is a Seine River Cruise. Whether you're celebrating a special occasion or simply soaking in the beauty of Paris, cruising along the Seine offers an entirely different perspective of the city's most famous landmarks. The river meanders through the heart of Paris, offering unobstructed views of some of the city's most famous monuments, including the Eiffel Tower, Notre-Dame Cathedral, and the Louvre.

Sightseeing Cruises: Classic Parisian Views

A sightseeing cruise along the Seine is one of the best ways to explore Paris at night. Most of these cruises last around an hour and offer detailed commentary, guiding you through the city's most famous sights while you relax on board. These tours are perfect for first-time visitors looking to get a comprehensive view of Paris's landmarks in a leisurely, scenic setting.

What to Expect: During the cruise, you'll float past illuminated monuments, including the Eiffel Tower, Pont Alexandre III, and Musée d'Orsay, while learning about Parisian history and culture. Many cruises depart from the Port de la Bourdonnais near the Eiffel Tower and offer additional options for dinner or drinks.

Best For: Those looking for a relaxed and scenic way to see the key sights of Paris while enjoying a comfortable, romantic atmosphere.

Dinner Cruises: A Culinary and Scenic Journey

For a more luxurious and romantic experience, a dinner cruise on the Seine is the ultimate way to combine gourmet dining with stunning views. As you cruise along the river, you'll enjoy a multi-course French meal, paired with fine wine, while the city's lights sparkle around you.

What to Expect: Most dinner cruises include a carefully curated menu featuring classic French dishes like foie gras, escargot, and crème brûlée. As you dine, you'll glide past Parisian landmarks illuminated at night, offering perfect photo opportunities. Many of these cruises offer live music or entertainment, adding to the festive atmosphere.

Best For: Couples or those celebrating a special occasion who want to experience the best of Paris's cuisine, culture, and romantic atmosphere all in one experience.

Private Cruises: Customized Parisian Experience

For a more exclusive and personalized experience, consider renting a private boat for your cruise along the Seine. These cruises can be tailored to your preferences, whether you're celebrating a special occasion, hosting a small event, or simply seeking a quiet, intimate experience of the river.

What to Expect: Private cruises can be arranged for groups of various sizes, and you may have the option to choose your route, dining options, and entertainment. Some even offer services like onboard chefs, personalized itineraries, and professional guides to help you explore the city in style.

Best For: Those looking for an intimate, customized experience, perfect for special events like birthdays, anniversaries, or proposals.

A Night to Remember in Paris

Whether you're seeking the glitz and glamour of a world-renowned cabaret or the tranquility and romance of a Seine river cruise, Paris offers a wealth of nighttime experiences that will leave you enchanted. From the glittering lights of the Eiffel Tower to the graceful arches of the Pont Neuf, these evening activities allow you to see a different side of the city—one filled with romance, history, and endless beauty.

Day Trips from Paris: Fontainebleau, Giverny, and Beyond

While Paris is undeniably captivating, the surrounding regions offer a wealth of day trip opportunities that provide a refreshing contrast to the hustle and bustle of the city. From royal châteaux to serene gardens and charming villages, there is much to explore just a short journey away. Here are two standout day trips from Paris that offer both historical intrigue and natural beauty.

Fontainebleau: A Royal Escape

A short 55-minute train ride from Paris will take you to the majestic town of Fontainebleau, home to the grand Château de Fontainebleau, one of the most impressive royal residences in France. Unlike the crowded palaces within Paris, Fontainebleau offers a more peaceful and immersive experience, allowing visitors to truly appreciate its historical significance.

What to See: The Château de Fontainebleau was the preferred residence of French monarchs from King Louis VII to Napoleon III. The château is a mix of Renaissance and classical French architecture, boasting more than 1,500 rooms filled with ornate decorations, grand staircases, and beautiful gardens. Highlights include the Gallery of Diana, the Grand Parterre gardens, and the Napoleon I Apartments, where Napoleon Bonaparte lived during his reign.

What to Do: Take a leisurely stroll through the extensive grounds, which include forested areas once used for royal hunting. Fontainebleau is also perfect for a picnic, as the surrounding forest is a designated UNESCO World Heritage Site and offers numerous scenic walking and cycling paths.

Best For: History lovers, architecture enthusiasts, and anyone who enjoys exploring beautiful gardens and tranquil settings.

Giverny: Monet's Garden Paradise

Just an hour away from Paris by train, Giverny is a small village that holds a special place in the heart of art lovers, thanks to the legendary Claude Monet. Giverny is the location of the artist's home and garden, where he spent the last 43 years of his life painting the iconic water lilies and other masterpieces that defined the Impressionist movement.

What to See: Monet's House and Gardens are the highlights of Giverny. The house, a charming property painted in pink, is surrounded by Monet's famous gardens, which are divided into two parts: the Flower Garden in front of the house and the Water Garden with its famous lily pond. Visitors can walk through the gardens, which appear exactly as Monet painted them, including the iconic Japanese bridge and weeping willows that feature prominently in his works.

What to Do: Spend time exploring the Monet Foundation, which houses many of Monet's works. After touring the gardens, wander around the peaceful village, enjoy lunch at a local bistro, or visit other art galleries dedicated to Impressionist artists.

Best For: Art aficionados, nature lovers, and anyone looking to experience a picturesque, tranquil escape from Paris.

Shopping in Paris: From Haute Couture to Vintage Finds

Paris has long been regarded as the fashion capital of the world, and its streets are a veritable treasure trove for those seeking the best in luxury, design, and style. Whether you're hunting for a high-end designer piece or seeking unique vintage finds, Paris offers a shopping experience like no other.

Haute Couture: The Pinnacle of Parisian Fashion

Paris is home to the world's most prestigious fashion houses, and a visit to the city would not be complete without experiencing the allure of haute couture. The luxury boutiques that line streets like the Avenue Montaigne and Rue du Faubourg Saint-Honoré showcase the very best of Parisian elegance and design.

What to See: Iconic fashion houses such as Chanel, Louis Vuitton, Dior, and Hermès all have flagship stores in Paris, where you can browse their latest collections, explore timeless classics, and indulge in one-of-a-kind couture pieces. For an unforgettable experience, you can even book a private appointment at one of these designer boutiques to receive personalized service.

What to Do: If haute couture is more about the experience than the purchase, consider attending a fashion show or exploring the Palais Galliera, the Museum of Fashion in Paris, which showcases the history of fashion through rotating exhibits of garments from the 18th century to the present.

Best For: Fashion enthusiasts, those seeking luxury shopping, and visitors wanting to immerse themselves in the world of high-end couture.

Vintage Finds: Hidden Gems and Unique Treasures

For those who prefer a more eclectic shopping experience, Paris is brimming with vintage shops and second-hand boutiques where you can find one-of-a-kind pieces that tell their own story. From leather goods to designer dresses, Paris's vintage stores offer a treasure hunt for the discerning shopper.

What to See: Areas like Le Marais and Montmartre are known for their abundance of vintage shops. Stores like Kiliwatch Paris and Le Relais de la Mode offer a curated selection of vintage clothing, shoes, and accessories, some of which feature high-end brands at a fraction of their original price.

What to Do: Take your time browsing through quirky boutiques like Chez Sarah and Marché aux Puces de Saint-Ouen, one of the largest flea markets in the world, located just outside Paris. Here, you can find antiques, vintage fashion, jewelry, and even rare collectibles. The market is a great place to spend an afternoon exploring stalls packed with unique finds.

Best For: Vintage lovers, bargain hunters, and anyone seeking a more personalized, one-of-a-kind shopping experience.

Department Stores and Concept Shops: Parisian Retail Excellence

If you're looking for a mix of modern retail with Parisian flair, head to the iconic Galeries Lafayette or Le Bon Marché, two of Paris's most famous department stores. These grand buildings offer everything from luxury goods to trendy fashion and gourmet foods.

What to See: Galeries Lafayette is famous for its stunning glass dome and its selection of high-end fashion, beauty products, and gourmet food. Le Bon Marché, the world's first department store, is known for its elegant atmosphere and curated selection of designer labels and artisanal products.

What to Do: Explore the diverse concept stores such as Colette, which merges fashion, art, and lifestyle in one space, or Merci, which offers a combination of home décor, fashion, and charity goods. Shopping in these venues allows you to explore the latest in Parisian design and trends, all under one roof.

Best For: Those looking for a blend of luxury, modern design, and curated shopping experiences.

Cooking Classes and Food Tours in Paris

Paris is renowned not only for its iconic landmarks and rich history but also for its exceptional cuisine. The city offers a wealth of opportunities to immerse yourself in the

French culinary tradition, whether through hands-on cooking classes or guided food tours. For food lovers and aspiring chefs alike, exploring Paris through its flavors can be a highlight of your trip. Here's how you can indulge in the city's gastronomic delights, both in the kitchen and on the streets.

Cooking Classes: Learn the Art of French Cuisine

There is no better way to truly understand the flavors of France than by taking part in a cooking class. Paris is home to a number of culinary schools and professional chefs offering lessons that range from quick introductory courses to full-day workshops. These classes not only teach you the technical skills needed to prepare French dishes but also provide a deeper understanding of the culture behind them.

Popular Cooking Classes in Paris

1. Le Cordon Bleu
As one of the most prestigious cooking schools in the world, Le Cordon Bleu offers a variety of cooking classes ranging from beginner to advanced levels. You'll learn techniques directly from world-class chefs and gain hands-on experience in preparing traditional French dishes. Whether it's a pastry workshop focusing on croissants and macarons or a class dedicated to classic French sauces, Le Cordon Bleu ensures a professional yet welcoming environment.

2. L'Atelier des Sens
Located in central Paris, L'Atelier des Sens is perfect for those who want to learn how to cook French cuisine in a relaxed and fun setting. Classes are offered in small groups, with an emphasis on practical, hands-on instruction. Their French cooking workshops cover everything from making soufflés and coq au vin to mastering the art of French patisserie.

3. La Cuisine Paris
For a more intimate cooking experience, La Cuisine Paris offers small-group lessons where you can learn to prepare traditional French dishes such as boeuf bourguignon, ratatouille, or tarte tatin. Classes are typically taught in English, making it accessible for all levels of French speakers. After the class, you get to enjoy the fruits of your labor

with a meal paired with wine, allowing you to savor the true taste of Parisian cuisine.

4. Cook'n with Class

Situated in the charming Montmartre area, Cook'n with Class offers a variety of hands-on classes, from market-to-table experiences to lessons focused on French baking or French wine and cheese pairings. Their French pastry classes are particularly popular, where you can learn to create pastries such as éclairs, madeleines, and macarons. The school prides itself on teaching practical skills that you can apply at home.

What You'll Learn

French Classics: Mastering iconic French dishes such as coq au vin, cassoulet, and quiche Lorraine.

Pastry and Baking: Learn how to make delicate macarons, flaky croissants, and tarte tatin.

Knife Skills and Techniques: French cuisine is all about precision and technique. Many classes focus on perfecting your knife skills and understanding the basic French cooking techniques like sautéing, poaching, and braising.

Wine Pairing: French food and wine go hand in hand. Many cooking schools offer specialized wine pairing classes that teach you how to match French wines with your meals.

Food Tours: A Taste of Parisian Neighborhoods

If you want to skip the stove and dive straight into Paris's culinary scene, a food tour is the way to go. Paris is made up of diverse neighborhoods, each with its own culinary specialties. A food tour will guide you through markets, bakeries, bistros, and chocolate shops, giving you the chance to taste authentic dishes and learn about Paris's food culture from an expert guide.

Popular Food Tours in Paris

1. Paris by Mouth

Paris by Mouth offers a variety of food tours, including walking tours of Le Marais, Saint -Germain-des-Prés, and Montmartre. These tours take you to local bakeries, cheese shops, chocolate boutiques, and wine cellars. You'll have the chance to sample fresh bread, creamy cheeses, decadent pastries, and fine wines. Guides are knowledgeable food experts who share stories and insights about the history of Parisian cuisine.

2. Secret Food Tours Paris

The Secret Food Tours offer a more off-the-beaten-path experience, taking you to hidden gems in the city that are beloved by locals but unknown to most tourists. Whether you're exploring the Latin Quarter or the Bastille, you'll taste French pâtisseries, explore bustling food markets, and enjoy lunch at a traditional bistro. The tours include tastings of local specialties like escargot, saucisson, and crêpes.

3. Bite of Paris Food Tours

If you're a fan of cheese and wine, Bite of Paris Food Tours has you covered with their cheese and wine-tasting tours. This tour lets you sample a range of French cheeses paired with hand-selected wines. You'll visit local fromageries, patisseries, and wine shops while learning about the origins and history of the French food you're tasting. It's a perfect tour for food lovers who want to understand the art of pairing.

4. Le Foodist

Le Foodist offers gourmet food tours and cooking classes, specializing in traditional French markets. You'll visit Marché des Enfants Rouges, the oldest covered market in Paris, and meet local food artisans to sample their products. The market-to-table tour ends with a cooking class where you'll prepare a meal with fresh ingredients you've picked up along the way.

What You'll Experience on a Food Tour

Sampling Local Specialties: From freshly baked baguettes and decadent chocolates to French cheeses and rich wines, you'll taste the best that Paris has to offer.

Hidden Culinary Gems: Discover Paris's culinary secrets, including artisanal bakeries, family-owned wine shops, and local food markets that most tourists never find.

Historical Insights: Learn about the history of French cuisine and how it's evolved, including the significance of ingredients like butter, cream, and herbs in traditional dishes.

Cultural Exploration: Gain a deeper understanding of Parisian food culture and how it's interwoven with the city's lifestyle and traditions.

Why You Should Try a Cooking Class or Food Tour

1. Authentic Experience: Whether cooking in a French kitchen or sampling delicacies at a local market, you'll experience Parisian food culture like a local.

2. Educational and Fun: These activities are an entertaining way to learn about French culinary traditions and pick up new skills.

3. Memorable Souvenirs: You'll leave with recipes, new techniques, and memories of the delicious meals and flavors you experienced.

4. Perfect for All Ages: Cooking classes and food tours are ideal for solo travelers, couples, and families looking to share an authentic Parisian experience.

Sleeping in Paris

Neighborhood Guide – Where to Stay

When planning a trip to Paris, choosing the right place to stay is crucial for an unforgettable experience. Paris is a sprawling city, and each neighborhood offers its own unique atmosphere, attractions, and accommodations. From the charming cobblestone streets of Montmartre to the chic elegance of the 7th arrondissement, there's a perfect area for every type of traveler. Whether you're a first-time visitor or a seasoned traveler, this guide will help you navigate Paris's diverse neighborhoods and find the ideal spot to call home during your stay.

1. Le Marais: Trendy, Historic, and Full of Life

Located in the heart of Paris, Le Marais is one of the most beloved neighborhoods for both tourists and locals. Known for its historic charm, cobbled streets, and vibrant arts scene, Le Marais offers a fantastic mix of traditional Parisian elements and modern flair. It's a great choice if you want to be close to major landmarks, like the Place des Vosges and Picasso Museum, but also enjoy trendy boutiques, lively cafés, and a diverse atmosphere.

Best For: Art lovers, history buffs, and foodies.

Accommodation: You'll find a mix of stylish boutique hotels, charming bed-and-breakfasts, and contemporary apartments.

Things to Do: Explore the historic Place des Vosges, visit the Musée Carnavalet for a deep dive into Parisian history, and shop in chic boutiques along Rue des Francs-Bourgeois.

2. Montmartre: Artistic and Bohemian

Famous for its artistic history and stunning views over the city, Montmartre is perfect for those who want to experience the more bohemian side of Paris. The neighborhood is centered around the iconic Sacré-Cœur Basilica, offering breathtaking views of the city from its hilltop location. In the late 19th and early 20th centuries, Montmartre was the heart of Paris's avant-garde artistic movement, and today it retains that creative charm with its artistic cafés, galleries, and cobblestone streets.

Best For: Art enthusiasts, couples, and those who want a more local, laid-back experience.

Accommodation: Stay in cozy boutique hotels, charming guesthouses, or Airbnb apartments with picturesque views of the basilica or surrounding streets.

Things to Do: Visit the Sacré-Cœur Basilica for stunning views, explore the Place du Tertre where artists sell their work, and discover the Musée de Montmartre.

3. Saint-Germain-des-Prés: Elegant and Literary

For a taste of Parisian sophistication and history, Saint-Germain-des-Prés in the 6th arrondissement is one of the most sought-after areas to stay. This chic neighborhood is known for its literary history, elegant cafés, and charming narrow streets. It's also home to Luxembourg Gardens, a peaceful escape from the city bustle, and numerous art galleries. A stay here offers a blend of intellectual and artistic vibes, with easy access to Paris's most famous attractions.

Best For: Culture seekers, romantics, and history enthusiasts.

Accommodation: Expect a mix of luxurious 5-star hotels, boutique stays, and stylish apartments with classic Parisian décor.

Things to Do: Take a walk through the Luxembourg Gardens, visit the Musée d'Orsay, and enjoy a coffee at the iconic Café de Flore.

4. The Latin Quarter: Historic and Vibrant

If you're looking for a more youthful and lively atmosphere, the Latin Quarter in the 5th arrondissement is a great option. Known for its historical significance as the center of intellectual and student life, the Latin Quarter is home to the Sorbonne University and some of Paris's most vibrant cafés and bookstores. The winding streets are filled with charming shops, lively bistros, and historical landmarks like the Panthéon and Jardin des Plantes.

Best For: Young travelers, history lovers, and those who enjoy a lively, youthful atmosphere.

Accommodation: The Latin Quarter offers a range of accommodations, including budget hotels, hostels, and more traditional guesthouses.

Things to Do: Visit the Panthéon, explore Rue Mouffetard for fresh produce and charming shops, and enjoy a picnic in the Jardin des Plantes.

5. The 7th Arrondissement: Classic Paris and the Eiffel Tower

If you dream of staying near the Eiffel Tower and experiencing the elegance of Paris, the 7th arrondissement is your perfect destination. This area exudes classic Parisian charm with wide avenues, beautiful architecture, and proximity to famous landmarks like the Musée d'Orsay and the Eiffel Tower. It's a quieter, more residential neighborhood that still offers plenty of opportunities for sightseeing and fine dining.

Best For: Couples, families, and those who want to stay near iconic landmarks.

Accommodation: The 7th is home to a range of luxurious hotels with views of the Eiffel Tower, as well as charming guesthouses.

Things to Do: Marvel at the Eiffel Tower, visit the Musée d'Orsay, and explore Rue Cler, a charming street full of food shops and cafés.

6. The 1st Arrondissement: Central and Convenient

For those who want to be in the heart of Paris, the 1st arrondissement offers the ultimate central location. Home to the Louvre Museum, Tuileries Gardens, and Palais Royal, staying here puts you just steps away from world-class art, shopping, and dining. The 1st arrondissement offers a more upscale experience but also provides easy access to other key areas of Paris.

Best For: First-time visitors, art lovers, and those seeking a central base for sightseeing.

Accommodation: You'll find a range of high-end hotels and apartments, as well as some luxury boutique options.

Things to Do: Visit the Louvre Museum, stroll through the Tuileries Gardens, and explore the luxury shops along the Rue de Rivoli.

7. Canal Saint-Martin: Hip and Trendy

For a more off-the-beaten-path experience, Canal Saint-Martin in the 10th arrondissement is one of Paris's trendiest neighborhoods. This area has become popular with the younger crowd, thanks to its mix of quirky boutiques, hip cafés, and a laid-back atmosphere along the canal. The area is also home to a growing number of stylish hotels and guesthouses, offering a more relaxed stay compared to the more traditional parts of Paris.

Best For: Young travelers, hipsters, and those looking for a unique Parisian experience.

Accommodation: From quirky boutique hotels to modern apartments, Canal Saint-Martin offers affordable options with a contemporary vibe.

Things to Do: Enjoy a leisurely stroll along the canal, visit the trendy shops and cafés, and check out the Marché Saint-Martin for local food and goods.

Finding Your Perfect Stay in Paris

Paris's diverse neighborhoods cater to every taste and budget, making it easy to find the perfect place to stay based on your interests and travel goals. Whether you prefer the historic charm of Le Marais, the artistic flair of Montmartre, or the elegance of the 7th arrondissement, there's an area that will make you feel at home while providing easy access to the city's world-famous sights. Your choice of neighborhood will shape your Parisian experience, so take the time to select an area that matches your style, interests, and the ambiance you want to enjoy during your stay in the City of Light.

Accommodation in Paris: Budget, Mid-Range, and Luxury Options

When visiting Paris, your choice of accommodation can significantly affect your experience, from how much you can explore to the atmosphere you'll enjoy. Whether you're a backpacker on a budget or seeking a lavish retreat, Paris has a wide range of accommodations to fit every need. Below are options for different budget categories to help you choose the right place to stay during your visit.

Budget Stays: Affordable Yet Comfortable

Paris can be an expensive city, but there are plenty of options for those on a budget that still provide comfort and convenience. Hostels, budget hotels, and guesthouses are great choices for travelers who want to enjoy Paris without breaking the bank. Many of these budget accommodations are located in central areas, giving you easy access to the city's top attractions.

Best Areas for Budget Stays:

The Latin Quarter: Known for its student vibe and affordable eateries, this area has many budget-friendly hotels and hostels.

Montmartre: Though it's a popular tourist spot, there are affordable options available here with charming local flair.

Belleville: This multicultural neighborhood offers budget accommodations, often with a more local, authentic feel.

Recommended Budget Stays:

Hostels: Generator Paris (Latin Quarter) is a trendy, budget-friendly choice offering dorm rooms and private rooms with a vibrant atmosphere.

Budget Hotels: Hotel de la Porte Dorée (12th arrondissement) provides clean, basic rooms at a great price with easy access to public transportation.

Guesthouses: Le Village Hostel (Montmartre) offers cozy, affordable rooms in a lively, youthful area.

Mid-Range Stays: Stylish Comfort Without the Price Tag

For those who want a balance of comfort and affordability, Paris offers a wide range of mid-range hotels and boutique accommodations. These options typically offer more amenities, stylish décor, and convenient locations without the premium price of luxury hotels. Whether you're traveling with family, friends, or as a couple, these stays provide a higher level of comfort and service.

Best Areas for Mid-Range Stays:

Le Marais: Known for its chic, trendy vibe, Le Marais offers a variety of stylish yet affordable boutique hotels.

Saint-Germain-des-Prés: This area is perfect for those who want to experience elegance and sophistication without the luxury price.

Canal Saint-Martin: A growing hotspot for young professionals and creatives, it offers unique accommodations with a bohemian touch.

Recommended Mid-Range Stays:

Hotel de la Bretonnerie (Le Marais): A charming boutique hotel that combines historical Parisian architecture with modern amenities.

Hotel d'Aubusson (Saint-Germain-des-Prés): A stylish hotel with a classic Parisian feel and a fantastic central location.

Hôtel Fabric (Canal Saint-Martin): A former textile factory turned boutique hotel, offering trendy rooms and a unique industrial chic design.

Luxury Stays: Indulgence and Elegance

For those looking to experience Paris at its finest, the city offers a range of luxury hotels that provide world-class service, unparalleled amenities, and stunning locations. From five-star hotels with sweeping views of the Eiffel Tower to opulent suites in historic buildings, luxury accommodations in Paris are perfect for travelers seeking a glamorous, once-in-a-lifetime experience.

Best Areas for Luxury Stays:

The 8th Arrondissement: This area, home to the Champs-Élysées and the Arc de Triomphe, is filled with high-end hotels offering luxury and convenience.

The 1st Arrondissement: With its proximity to iconic landmarks like the Louvre and Tuileries Gardens, this area features some of the best luxury hotels in Paris.

The 7th Arrondissement: For those who want to be near the Eiffel Tower and enjoy elegant surroundings, this area offers exclusive hotels and palatial accommodations.

Recommended Luxury Stays:

Le Meurice (1st Arrondissement): A legendary 5-star hotel with classic French elegance, exceptional dining, and a spa fit for royalty.

Shangri-La Hotel Paris (7th Arrondissement): An opulent palace hotel with magnificent views of the Eiffel Tower and impeccable service.

The Ritz Paris (8th Arrondissement): One of the most iconic hotels in the world, offering unrivaled luxury, historic grandeur, and world-class dining.

Unique Stays: Boutique Hotels and Airbnb Gems

For travelers looking for something truly special, Paris offers a wealth of boutique hotels and Airbnb properties that provide personalized, distinctive experiences. These unique accommodations often reflect the character and charm of the neighborhoods they are located in and can be an excellent alternative to traditional hotels.

Boutique Hotels: Paris with Character

Boutique hotels in Paris offer a more intimate, personalized stay. These smaller, independent hotels are known for their distinctive style, cozy atmospheres, and creative interiors. Many boutique hotels in Paris blend modern comforts with traditional French charm, making them a great choice for travelers who want to experience a more authentic, unique side of the city.

Recommended Boutique Hotels:

Hotel Henriette (Latin Quarter): A stylish boutique hotel with a vintage, retro flair, offering a cozy, artistic vibe and a great location.

Hotel Panache (9th Arrondissement): A charming hotel with Art Deco-inspired décor and a lively atmosphere, perfect for a more quirky, stylish stay.

Le Petit Paris (Latin Quarter): A beautifully designed boutique hotel with a warm, welcoming feel and luxurious rooms in a central location.

Airbnb Gems: A Home Away from Home

Airbnb has revolutionized the way people travel, offering a range of unique properties that can give you a more personal, home-like experience in Paris. Whether you're staying in an elegant Haussmannian apartment, a trendy loft in the Marais, or a charming studio near the Eiffel Tower, Airbnb offers the flexibility of choosing from a wide range of options that cater to various tastes and budgets.

Best Areas for Airbnb Stays:

Le Marais: With its narrow streets and historical charm, Le Marais has some of the most unique and stylish Airbnb properties, from rustic apartments to chic modern studios.

Montmartre: Experience Paris like a local with an Airbnb in Montmartre, surrounded by cafés, artists, and cobbled streets.

The 11th Arrondissement: A lesser-known area with a bohemian vibe, this neighborhood offers a more affordable option for those looking to stay in a more local environment.

Recommended Airbnb Stays:

A charming artist's loft in the Marais, complete with exposed brick walls and vintage furnishings, offering a true Parisian experience.

A luxurious penthouse near the Eiffel Tower, with a terrace offering stunning views of the landmark.

A quaint studio apartment in Montmartre, just steps from the iconic Sacré-Cœur, providing a cozy escape in one of Paris's most picturesque neighborhoods.

Finding Your Ideal Stay in Paris

Whether you're traveling on a budget, seeking mid-range comfort, or indulging in luxury, Paris has a wide variety of accommodations to fit every need and style. For a more intimate experience, boutique hotels and unique Airbnb properties offer a chance to experience the city in a personalized way, while traditional hotels provide convenience and comfort. Whichever type of stay you choose, Paris offers something for every traveler, ensuring that your visit will be unforgettable from the moment you check in.

Tips for Booking Accommodations in Paris

Booking accommodations in Paris can be an exciting yet daunting task, with so many options to choose from across various neighborhoods. To help make the process smoother and ensure you find the perfect place for your stay, here are some practical tips to guide your booking process.

1. Book Early, Especially for Peak Seasons

Paris is one of the most popular tourist destinations in the world, and accommodations can fill up quickly, especially during peak travel seasons (spring and summer, holidays like Christmas and New Year's, or special events such as Paris Fashion Week). To secure the best deals and avoid limited availability, it's highly recommended to book your accommodation at least 2-3 months in advance, especially if you're visiting during high season.

2. Research the Neighborhoods Thoroughly

Paris is a city of diverse neighborhoods, each with its own unique charm and atmosphere. Choosing the right area can enhance your experience, whether you want to be close to major attractions, find local cafés, or stay in a quieter residential area. Here are some tips for choosing your perfect neighborhood:

For first-time visitors: Stay near central districts like the 1st (Louvre) or 7th (Eiffel Tower) if you want easy access to major attractions.

For a local vibe: Consider neighborhoods like Le Marais (historic and trendy) or Canal Saint-Martin (bohemian and vibrant).

For a romantic atmosphere: The Latin Quarter and Montmartre are iconic for their charming, intimate feel.

For quiet stays: If you prefer less hustle and bustle, consider the 11th or 12th Arrondissements, which are more residential but still well-connected to the city center.

By understanding the different neighborhoods, you can book a stay that suits your travel style and proximity to the sights you wish to explore.

3. Consider Your Transportation Options

Paris has an extensive and efficient public transportation system, including the Métro, buses, and trams. When booking your accommodation, make sure to check how close your hotel or rental is to a Métro station or major transit lines. This can save you time and energy when traveling between sights. For those traveling from airports, it's also wise to check if your accommodation is easily accessible by public transport or if it's close to an airport shuttle or taxi stand.

Proximity to a Métro station can make all the difference, as it allows you to explore different parts of the city quickly and easily.

Walking distance to major attractions like the Louvre or Notre-Dame is ideal if you prefer to explore by foot.

4. Read Reviews and Ratings

Before confirming any booking, take the time to read reviews on trusted sites such as TripAdvisor, Booking.com, or Airbnb. Look for recent guest feedback that highlights the cleanliness, service quality, and location of the accommodation. Pay attention to common themes in the reviews, such as:

Customer service: Are the hosts or hotel staff friendly and responsive?

Cleanliness and comfort: Is the place clean, well-maintained, and comfortable?

Value for money: Does the price match the quality of the stay?

Reviews can also provide insight into potential issues like noise, lack of amenities, or hidden fees, helping you make an informed decision.

5. Watch Out for Hidden Fees

Some accommodations in Paris, especially on platforms like Airbnb, might have hidden fees that aren't included in the advertised price. These can include cleaning fees, service charges, or extra costs for amenities (such as internet access, laundry services, or early check-in).

Check the total cost before booking to avoid surprises at checkout.

For hotels, taxes may not be included in the initial price, so ensure you confirm the final price.

Airbnb: Always check for extra charges like cleaning fees, guest fees, or any deposit requirements.

6. Choose the Right Type of Accommodation

Paris offers a wide variety of accommodation types, each providing a different experience. When booking, consider what type of stay best fits your preferences and travel goals:

Boutique Hotels: For those who want personalized service and unique décor.

Hostels: Ideal for budget travelers or those looking to meet fellow tourists.

Hotels: Great for standard comfort and services in central locations.

Airbnb: Offers flexibility and local experience, especially for longer stays or those looking for apartment-style accommodations.

7. Pay Attention to Room Features and Amenities

When booking a hotel or Airbnb, always check what amenities are included in the room or property. Some important features to consider:

Wi-Fi access: Essential for travelers who need to stay connected.

Air-conditioning or heating: Paris can be hot in the summer or chilly in the winter, so make sure your accommodation offers the right climate control.

Breakfast options: Some hotels offer breakfast included in the room rate, while others might have an extra charge.

Kitchen or kitchenette: For longer stays or those looking to save on meals, having a kitchen can be convenient.

8. Look for Deals and Special Offers

Paris can be pricey, but with a bit of research, you can find discounts and promotions on accommodations. Here are a few ways to save:

Use discount platforms: Websites like Booking.com, Hotels.com, and Expedia often offer special deals or discounts.

Book directly with hotels: Some hotels offer better rates or free perks (such as breakfast or early check-in) when you book directly through their websites.

Check for last-minute deals: Websites like HotelTonight specialize in offering last-minute accommodation deals, which can be ideal for spontaneous travelers.

9. Double-Check Your Reservation

After booking, make sure to review the reservation details to confirm everything is correct. This includes the check-in time, payment details, and any special requests (like late check-in, early check-out, or room preferences).

Confirm with the property: A few days before your trip, it's always a good idea to confirm your booking with the hotel or Airbnb host, especially during peak seasons when accommodations are in high demand.

Cancellation policy: Be aware of the cancellation terms, in case plans change. Flexible cancellation policies allow for easier changes or refunds.

10. Consider the Season and Local Events

Paris hosts a variety of events throughout the year, from festivals to exhibitions. If you're traveling during a popular event, accommodations may fill up quickly, and prices may rise. Consider checking the event calendar for Paris before you book to ensure you're not caught off guard by higher demand.

Summer (June-August): High season with tourists flocking to see the sights. Prices tend to be higher, and popular accommodations can book out months in advance.

Winter (November-February): A quieter time to visit, with lower prices, fewer crowds, and a more intimate Parisian experience.

Spring (March-May) and Autumn (September-November): Great times to visit with mild weather, fewer crowds, and moderate prices.

Eating

Classic French Cuisine and Must-Try Dishes

Paris is synonymous with gastronomic excellence, where rich culinary traditions meet modern innovation. From timeless bistros to Michelin-starred restaurants, the city offers a dazzling array of flavors, textures, and experiences for food lovers. Here are some of the most iconic dishes you must try during your visit to the French capital.

1. Croissant

No visit to Paris is complete without indulging in a freshly baked croissant. This golden, flaky pastry is a breakfast staple, often enjoyed with a café au lait. A classic French croissant is made from buttery, laminated dough that creates its signature layers.

Where to Try: Look for a local bakery (boulangerie) to experience the best croissants. Famous bakeries like Pierre Hermé and Du Pain et des Idées serve some of the finest examples.

2. Baguette

The quintessential symbol of French bread, the baguette is a long, slender loaf with a crispy crust and soft, airy interior. It's often eaten with cheese, pâté, or jam. The French take great pride in their baguettes, and you'll find them in every boulangerie across Paris.

Where to Try: Any traditional bakery will have a baguette, but Le Grenier à Pain is particularly famous for its artisanal approach to this iconic bread.

3. Escargots de Bourgogne (Snails)

For the adventurous eater, escargots de Bourgogne are a true French delicacy. Snails are cooked in a rich garlic butter sauce with parsley and sometimes a hint of wine, making them surprisingly delicious. The snails are tender, and the garlic butter sauce is perfect for dipping crusty bread.

Where to Try: L'Escargot Montorgueil is a classic Parisian restaurant known for its escargots and traditional French fare.

4. Coq au Vin

A hearty and comforting dish, coq au vin is made by slow-cooking chicken in red wine, usually with mushrooms, onions, and sometimes bacon. The slow braising process infuses the meat with rich flavors, making it a satisfying dish for colder months or a relaxed evening meal.

Where to Try: Le Comptoir du Relais in the 6th arrondissement serves a delicious, traditional coq au vin.

5. Duck Confit (Confit de Canard)

Confit de canard is a classic French dish where duck legs are slow-cooked in their own fat until tender and golden brown on the outside. The result is a savory, melt-in-your-mouth experience with crispy skin and juicy meat. It's often served with roasted potatoes or vegetables.

Where to Try: For a perfect confit de canard, head to Le Gastronome or Chez L'Ami Jean.

6. Ratatouille

A quintessential vegetable stew from Provence, ratatouille is made from a medley of summer vegetables like tomatoes, zucchini, eggplant, and bell peppers, slowly cooked in olive oil and herbs. This dish is both healthy and flavorful, offering a true taste of southern France.

Where to Try: For an authentic version, try Chez Janou, a lively bistro in the Marais district.

7. Soupe à l'Oignon (French Onion Soup)

Soupe à l'oignon is a beloved French comfort food, particularly in winter. Made with caramelized onions, rich broth, and topped with a cheesy crouton, this dish is both savory and satisfying. The rich flavor comes from the long cooking process of the onions, which develop a deep, sweet profile.

Where to Try: Le Procope, one of Paris's oldest cafés, offers an excellent rendition of this classic dish.

8. Foie Gras

A luxury French dish, foie gras is made from the liver of a duck or goose, prepared with rich spices and served either as pâté, mousse, or simply pan-seared. Often paired with sweet accompaniments like fig jam or a glass of Sauternes wine, it's a decadent dish for special occasions.

Where to Try: Maison Troisgros offers an upscale dining experience with exceptional foie gras.

9. Quiche Lorraine

Originating from the Lorraine region, quiche lorraine is a savory tart made with eggs, cream, and bacon, often flavored with cheese and herbs. It's perfect for a light lunch or a picnic in one of Paris's parks, served either warm or at room temperature.

Where to Try: Head to Le Pain Quotidien for a hearty slice or try Boucherie Moderne for a more traditional take.

10. Crêpes

Whether savory or sweet, crêpes are a beloved French treat. The savory variety (called galettes) is made with buckwheat flour and filled with ingredients like cheese, ham, and eggs. Sweet crêpes are made with white flour and can be filled with anything from Nutella and bananas to lemon and sugar.

Where to Try: Crêperie Josselin in the Montparnasse district is renowned for its excellent crêpes, particularly the savory ones.

11. Tarte Tatin

A famous French dessert, tarte tatin is an upside-down apple tart where the apples are caramelized in butter and sugar before being baked under a flaky pastry crust. When inverted, the result is a beautifully golden and sweet treat that's both comforting and indulgent.

Where to Try: Café Constant and Le Soufflé are both known for their delightful tarte tatin.

12. Cheese (Fromage)

France is famous for its cheese, with over 400 varieties to choose from. You'll encounter many types, including brie (soft and creamy), camembert (pungent and rich), and comté (nutty and firm). Typically, cheese is served at the end of a meal with a selection of bread or fruit.

Where to Try: Visit Fromagerie Laurent Dubois for a curated selection of high-quality cheeses.

13. Wine Pairing

No French meal is complete without wine. France is home to some of the world's best vineyards, and each region offers its own specialties. Bordeaux is known for its reds, Chablis for its whites, and Champagne is famous for its bubbly. Ask your waiter for pairing suggestions based on the dishes you order.

Where to Try: Many bistros and brasseries will offer wine pairings with meals, but for a refined experience, visit Le Cinq at the Four Seasons Hotel George V, where expert sommeliers guide you through exquisite wine pairings.

14. Parisian Pastries: Eclairs, Madeleines, and Macarons

When in Paris, don't forget to sample the incredible pastries the city is famous for. Éclairs (choux pastry filled with cream and topped with chocolate) are a must-try, as are delicate madeleines (small sponge cakes) and vibrant macarons (meringue-based cookies filled with ganache).

Where to Try: For macaroons, visit Pierre Hermé or Ladurée, both known for their expertly crafted, colorful macarons.

15. Café Culture

Finally, a trip to Paris wouldn't be complete without experiencing the iconic café culture. Whether you're sipping an espresso or indulging in a café crème, take the time to sit at a sidewalk café, watch the world go by, and enjoy the simple pleasure of Parisian café life.

Where to Try: Café de Flore and Les Deux Magots in Saint-Germain-des-Prés are two of the most famous cafés in Paris, steeped in history.

Best Bistros, Brasseries, and Michelin-Starred Restaurants in Paris

Paris is a city where dining is not just a meal—it's an experience. Whether you're seeking a classic French bistro, a lively brasserie, or an unforgettable Michelin-starred experience, Paris offers a range of dining options that cater to every taste and budget. Here's a guide to some of the best establishments in the city.

Bistros: Classic Parisian Charm

A bistro is an essential part of Parisian culture, offering simple, hearty dishes served in a relaxed, yet intimate setting. These establishments often emphasize fresh, locally sourced ingredients and are perfect for a casual yet authentic French meal.

Le Comptoir du Relais (6th arrondissement): A quintessential bistro that blends traditional French fare with modern twists. The restaurant's duck confit and seafood dishes are especially popular. Its charming ambiance makes it a perfect choice for a relaxed meal after a day of sightseeing.

Bistro Paul Bert (11th arrondissement): Famous for its classic French dishes, this bistro is renowned for its steak frites and rich, flavorful sauces. Its traditional approach to French cuisine makes it a favorite among locals and visitors alike.

Le Bistrot d'Henri (7th arrondissement): With a cozy, Parisian ambiance, this bistro offers classic dishes like escargots, duck breast, and chocolate mousse. The attentive service and intimate setting make it a wonderful choice for a laid-back dinner.

Brasseries: Casual Dining with a Touch of Glamour

A brasserie is a more expansive, bustling establishment where guests can enjoy traditional French dishes in a slightly more lively atmosphere than a bistro. Here, you'll find a wider selection of drinks and often a more extensive menu.

Bofinger (11th arrondissement): One of the oldest and most iconic brasseries in Paris, Bofinger offers an extensive menu of French classics in a grand setting. Known for its seafood platters and sauerkraut dishes, it's a great place for those craving a true brasserie experience.

Brasserie Lipp (6th arrondissement): A Paris institution, this brasserie has been serving Parisian classics like choucroute, oysters, and roast meats since 1880. The Art Deco interior adds to the charm, and it's a perfect spot to immerse yourself in Parisian history while dining.

La Coupole (Montparnasse): A legendary brasserie with a glamorous interior, La Coupole serves up hearty portions of traditional French fare. Known for its shellfish platters, coq au vin, and rich seafood dishes, it's perfect for a festive meal.

Michelin-Starred Restaurants: A Gourmet Experience

For those seeking the pinnacle of fine dining, Paris boasts numerous Michelin-starred restaurants that offer unparalleled culinary experiences. From exquisite tasting menus to meticulously crafted dishes, dining at one of these establishments is a once-in-a-lifetime experience.

Le Meurice (1st arrondissement): This three-star Michelin restaurant is helmed by renowned chef Alain Ducasse and offers an extraordinary dining experience. The modern French cuisine with a twist of innovation is paired with an elegant atmosphere, making it an unforgettable experience.

L'Arpège (7th arrondissement): With three Michelin stars, L'Arpège is a temple of modern French cuisine, renowned for its creative use of vegetables. Chef Alain Passard is famous for elevating produce to center stage, offering extraordinary dishes that highlight seasonality and flavor in new ways.

Le Bernardin (4th arrondissement): Known for its outstanding seafood, Le Bernardin is a Michelin-starred restaurant that combines French culinary techniques with a modern touch. The tasting menus and fish-focused dishes are elegantly prepared and presented, offering a gourmet experience worth savoring.

Guy Savoy (6th arrondissement): A bastion of classic French haute cuisine, this three-star Michelin restaurant serves luxurious French dishes with a modern twist. Guy Savoy's famous artichoke soup and lobster dishes are signature options on an extraordinary menu that celebrates French culinary traditions.

Budget-Friendly Dining Options in Paris

While Paris is often associated with luxury dining experiences, the city also offers a wide variety of budget-friendly options that provide exceptional quality at a more affordable price. Whether you're craving a quick bite or a leisurely lunch, these spots will satisfy your taste buds without breaking the bank.

1. Crêperies: Quick, Delicious, and Affordable

A crêpe is one of the most iconic street foods in Paris, and it's also a budget-friendly option. From savory galettes filled with ham, cheese, and eggs to sweet crêpes drizzled with Nutella or jam, these treats are perfect for a quick meal.

Crêperie Josselin (Montparnasse): This family-run crêperie offers savory buckwheat galettes and sweet crêpes. The quality is exceptional, and the prices are reasonable for the generous portions.

Crêperie Bretonne (5th arrondissement): For a traditional French crêpe experience, head to this quaint spot near the Latin Quarter. The menu offers a variety of options, from simple sugar crêpes to hearty filled ones.

2. Casual Bistros and Brasseries

Not every bistro or brasserie in Paris comes with a hefty price tag. In fact, many smaller, family-run spots serve up delicious meals at affordable prices, especially in less touristy areas.

Le Petit Cler (7th arrondissement): Located on the charming Rue Cler, this bistro offers traditional French dishes at a reasonable price. Enjoy a delicious quiche or a light salad niçoise for an affordable meal.

Chez René (5th arrondissement): Famous for its hearty French fare, this casual bistro serves up dishes like cassoulet and pot-au-feu without the high price tag of more upscale spots.

3. Fast Casual Options

For those in a rush or looking for a quick bite without sacrificing quality, Paris is full of gourmet fast food options that serve high-quality French sandwiches, salads, and pastries.

L'As du Fallafel (Marais): A legendary stop for falafel and Middle Eastern specialties, L'As du Fallafel serves hearty portions of falafel in pita, stuffed with fresh ingredients and sauces, all at a reasonable price.

Le Relais de l'Entrecôte (Multiple locations): If you're craving a hearty steak and fries, this chain offers entrecôte steak served with a secret sauce and frites at a great price. It's a simple, no-frills option that delivers a satisfying meal.

4. Market and Street Food

For the ultimate budget-friendly dining experience, explore Paris's street markets or grab something from one of the many food trucks or stands. Markets like Marché d'Aligre and Marché des Enfants Rouges offer fresh produce, cheeses, cured meats, and ready-to-eat meals like rotisserie chicken or tartines (open-faced sandwiches), perfect for a picnic in one of Paris's beautiful parks.

5. Bakeries and Patisseries

Many of Paris's finest bakeries offer affordable yet delicious options, ranging from freshly baked baguettes to pastries and sandwiches.

Boulangerie Poilâne (6th arrondissement): This iconic bakery serves up delicious pain de campagne, sandwiches, and sweet pastries at reasonable prices. Grab a quick snack or take a loaf of bread with you for a picnic in the park.

Maison Pichard (15th arrondissement): Known for its brioche and tartes, this bakery offers a range of sweet and savory pastries that make for a satisfying breakfast or lunch on the go.

Parisian Cafés and Bakery Highlights

Paris is synonymous with cafés and bakeries, each offering a distinct experience of French culture, from sipping an espresso on a sunlit terrace to savoring a flaky croissant in a charming patisserie. These spots aren't just places to eat—they're an integral part of the Parisian lifestyle, offering locals and visitors alike a taste of tradition and ambiance. Below are some of the best cafés and bakeries in Paris, each with its own unique flair.

1. Classic Parisian Cafés: Sipping in Style

A café in Paris is more than a place to drink coffee—it's an essential cultural ritual. The atmosphere, people-watching, and experience are just as important as the drink itself. Paris boasts a variety of cafés that offer a quintessential Parisian experience.

Café de Flore (6th arrondissement)

One of the oldest and most iconic cafés in Paris, Café de Flore has been a popular haunt for intellectuals, artists, and writers since 1887. The Art Deco interior, paired with the sidewalk terrace, makes it an ideal spot for sipping an espresso and watching the world go by. Try the croissant or the omelette au fromage for a true Parisian breakfast.

Les Deux Magots (6th arrondissement)

Located just a few steps away from Café de Flore, Les Deux Magots is another legendary café that has attracted famous figures such as Simone de Beauvoir and Ernest Hemingway. With its vintage ambiance and classic menu, it's perfect for a coffee break while exploring the Saint-Germain-des-Prés area. Enjoy a café crème alongside a pain au chocolat for a classic pairing.

Café de la Paix (9th arrondissement)

Overlooking the Opéra Garnier, this historic café offers a lavish and elegant setting, making it ideal for a more refined café experience. Famous for its grand interior and iconic Parisian pastries, this café is a great place to relax and indulge in a cup of coffee or a hot chocolate, especially after a performance at the opera.

2. Hidden Gem Cafés: Off-the-Beaten-Path Delights

For those who want to escape the crowds and enjoy a more intimate Parisian café experience, there are plenty of hidden gems tucked away in the city's neighborhoods. These cafés offer a quieter, cozier environment, perfect for relaxing with a book or engaging in conversation.

Le Progrès (3rd arrondissement)

Nestled in the heart of the Le Marais, Le Progrès is a charming café that exudes Parisian charm. With its vintage décor and laid-back atmosphere, it's a great spot for a leisurely afternoon. Order a café au lait and pair it with a freshly made quiche lorraine for a light meal.

Café Charlot (3rd arrondissement)

A traditional French café with a vintage vibe, Café Charlot offers both classic and creative dishes in an unpretentious setting. Located near the Canal Saint-Martin, it's the perfect spot to enjoy a latte while watching the world go by. The outdoor seating area is great for people-watching.

Café des Deux Moulins (18th arrondissement)

Made famous by the movie Amélie, this charming café in Montmartre is a must-visit for fans of the film. With its quirky interior and friendly vibe, it offers a unique, off-the-beaten-path experience. Enjoy a café noisette (espresso with a dash of hazelnut) and a tarte tatin for dessert while taking in the iconic Parisian atmosphere.

3. Iconic Parisian Bakeries: A Taste of Tradition

Paris is home to some of the finest bakeries in the world, where the art of French baking has been passed down through generations. From buttery croissants to perfect baguettes, these bakeries serve up the finest pastries that define Parisian gastronomy.

Maison Pichard (15th arrondissement)

Regarded as one of the best bakeries in Paris, Maison Pichard is famous for its exceptional brioche, tartes, and viennoiseries. The bakery has been awarded the title of Meilleur Ouvrier de France, a prestigious title that recognizes the best craftsmen in France. Try their famous brioche à tête or their rich chocolate éclair for a sweet treat.

Le Grenier à Pain (18th arrondissement)

A top-rated bakery in Paris, Le Grenier à Pain has won numerous awards for its exceptional bread, particularly its baguettes. The bakery's rustic yet modern feel makes it a delightful stop while strolling through Montmartre. Be sure to grab a fresh baguette or one of their delicate pastries like a pistachio éclair.

Pierre Hermé (6th arrondissement)

Known for his innovative takes on French pastries, Pierre Hermé is a must-visit for pastry lovers. His macarons are legendary, with flavors ranging from rose to pistachio and salted caramel. The Ispahan macaron—featuring rose, lychee, and raspberry—is a signature creation that should not be missed. Pair it with a café gourmand to experience a variety of mini desserts with your coffee.

4. Unique French Pastries and Desserts

When in Paris, indulging in traditional French pastries is a must. Here are some of the most iconic treats to try at Parisian cafés and bakeries:

Croissant

No visit to Paris is complete without a buttery croissant. The golden, flaky pastry is perfect for breakfast, paired with a hot coffee. The best croissants are often found at neighborhood bakeries where the dough is made fresh daily.

Pain au Chocolat

A favorite of both locals and tourists, pain au chocolat is a croissant-like pastry filled with a rich bar of dark chocolate. It's a delicious breakfast treat or afternoon snack.

Macarons

These delicate, colorful meringue-based cookies filled with creamy ganache are a must-try in Paris. The best macarons are from renowned pastry chefs like Pierre Hermé and Ladurée, both of which offer a wide array of flavors.

Tarte Tatin

This upside-down caramelized apple tart is a classic French dessert. The perfect balance of sweet and tart, with a buttery pastry base, makes it a favorite in Parisian cafés. Don't forget to pair it with a strong espresso or café crème.

Éclairs

A traditional French dessert, the éclair is a long, filled pastry, usually with cream or chocolate filling. It's topped with a glossy layer of icing, making it as visually appealing as it is delicious. Try variations like coffee, chocolate, or vanilla at any Parisian patisserie.

5. Cafés and Bakery Etiquette

While enjoying your Parisian café or bakery experience, keep in mind a few local tips:

Seating: In cafés, it's common to sit at a table even if you're just having a coffee. Expect to pay a little extra if you opt to sit at a terrace table, as the prices are higher than at the counter.

Tipping: Tipping is appreciated but not obligatory in Paris. A small tip (around 5-10%) is often left if service is good, though it's included in your bill.

Takeaway: If you're on the go, most bakeries offer takeaway options, but it's often nice to pause and enjoy your treats in a nearby park or at a café table.

Pace Yourself: Parisian cafés are meant for relaxing. Don't rush—enjoy your coffee, watch the world go by, and take in the Parisian atmosphere.

Practicalities

Getting Around Paris

Paris is a city that encourages exploration, and with its efficient transportation system, getting from one iconic sight to another is a breeze. Whether you prefer the underground charm of the metro, the freedom of biking through picturesque streets, or the timeless simplicity of walking, Paris offers a variety of ways to experience its beauty. Here's an extensive guide on how to navigate Paris and make the most of your time in this enchanting city.

1. The Paris Métro: Fast and Efficient

The Paris Metro is one of the most convenient ways to travel around the city. Operating since 1900, the metro has 16 lines that cover nearly every part of Paris, from the grand boulevards to quieter residential districts. Whether you're visiting famous landmarks or heading to a lesser-known museum, the metro is often your quickest option.

How to Use the Metro

The Paris Metro is easy to use, even for first-time visitors. Tickets can be purchased from machines or ticket counters at metro stations. You'll need a T+ ticket for single journeys, which allows you to transfer between metro lines and buses, as well as travel on the RER within central Paris zones. You can also purchase a Paris Visite pass for unlimited travel over several days, which offers great value if you plan to do a lot of sightseeing.

Stations and Lines: The metro system is color-coded, with each line represented by a number and a corresponding color on the map. Be sure to check the final destination on the platform sign to ensure you're heading in the right direction.

Accessibility: Many metro stations are equipped with escalators or elevators, but not all are fully accessible. If you have mobility issues, check the station's facilities in advance or opt for the bus system, which is more accessible.

Key Metro Tips

Avoid rush hours: The metro can get crowded during peak hours (8:00–9:00 AM and 5:00–7:00 PM), so if possible, try to travel during off-peak times for a more comfortable ride.

Stay alert: Pickpocketing can be an issue in crowded metro cars, so keep your belongings close and be aware of your surroundings.

2. Parisian Buses: Scenic and Relaxed

While the metro is fast, Parisian buses offer a more scenic and relaxed way to travel. Buses crisscross the city, allowing you to enjoy the sights while you travel. Riding a bus offers an entirely different perspective of Paris, as you pass by charming streets, bustling squares, and hidden corners of the city.

How to Use the Bus

Like the metro, buses operate on the T+ ticket system, which can be used for single rides or transfers. You can also use a Paris Visite pass for unlimited bus travel. Buses run from 7:00 AM to 8:30 PM, and night buses (known as Noctilien) operate from 12:30 AM to 5:30 AM on major routes.

Bus Stops: Buses stop at designated points along their route. You can find the schedule at bus stops, and it's a good idea to arrive a few minutes early to avoid missing your bus.

Routes and Destinations: The bus network covers all areas of Paris, including areas not served by the metro. Popular routes like the Line 69 (which passes through Montmartre and the Latin Quarter) and the Line 72 (which runs along the Seine, passing the Eiffel Tower and Musée d'Orsay) offer a picturesque tour of the city.

Key Bus Tips

Be patient: Buses can be slower than the metro due to traffic. Allow extra time to reach your destination, especially during busy hours.

Check the schedules: Buses may not run as frequently in some areas or at night, so make sure to check the departure times before heading to the bus stop.

3. Biking in Paris: A Sustainable and Fun Option

Paris is increasingly becoming a bike-friendly city, with many bike lanes and dedicated cycling paths weaving through the streets. Cycling through Paris is an enjoyable and sustainable way to explore the city, giving you the freedom to stop at any charming café or hidden park you spot along the way.

Bike Rental Services: Vélib'

The Vélib' bike-sharing system is the most popular way for visitors to rent a bike in Paris. With over 1,400 stations and around 20,000 bikes available throughout the city, it's easy to pick up a bike and ride around. You can choose between traditional bicycles or electric bikes for a more effortless ride.

Renting a Bike: You can rent a bike using the Vélib' app or at any Vélib' station, where you can pay by card or with a Vélib' pass. There are both short-term and long-term rental options, so you can rent a bike for a few hours or an entire day.

Bike Lanes: Paris has an extensive network of bike lanes, especially in central areas like the Marais and Latin Quarter, making it safe and easy to navigate. Look out for the green bike lane signs to stay on track.

Key Cycling Tips

Stay in bike lanes: Though the city is bike-friendly, always stay within designated bike lanes for your safety.

Use the bike app: The Vélib' app will show you the locations of bike stations, so you can easily find one near your destination or find a vacant bike to rent.

Be aware of traffic: Paris is a bustling city, and while bike lanes are available, you'll still need to be mindful of cars, pedestrians, and other cyclists.

4. Walking: The Best Way to Experience Paris

Paris is a walking city, and some of the most enchanting experiences are found when you explore on foot. Strolling down narrow alleyways, crossing cobblestone streets, and taking in the stunning architecture are all part of the charm of Paris. Many of the city's most famous sights, like the Louvre, Notre-Dame, and the Champs-Élysées, are best enjoyed on foot.

Walking Tours

Walking tours are a fantastic way to experience the city, especially if you're short on time and want to make sure you don't miss any hidden gems. There are various options available, from guided walking tours through historic neighborhoods to self-guided tours using an app or guidebook.

Walk in the Tuileries Gardens: A leisurely stroll through the Tuileries Gardens offers an excellent introduction to Parisian style, with neatly manicured lawns, fountains, and sculptures. It's an ideal spot for a break after visiting the Louvre.

Explore Montmartre: The bohemian Montmartre neighborhood is full of winding streets, staircases, and hidden squares. Walking through this historic area lets you soak up the artistic atmosphere of Paris, with quaint cafés, artists' studios, and the iconic Sacré-Cœur Basilica at the top of the hill.

Key Walking Tips

Wear comfortable shoes: Parisian streets, especially in areas like Le Marais and Montmartre, can be uneven or cobbled, so comfortable shoes are a must.

Take breaks: Paris is a city meant to be savored, so don't rush your walk. Take time to relax in one of the many parks or cafés along your route.

Use a map or GPS: While Paris is relatively easy to navigate, it's always a good idea to have a map or GPS handy in case you wander off the beaten path.

5. Taxis and Ride-Hailing: Convenient but Expensive

Taxis are readily available throughout Paris, but they can be more expensive compared to the metro or buses. If you're in a hurry or need a direct route to your destination, a taxi or ride-hailing service like Uber can be a convenient option.

Taxis: Official Paris taxis can be hailed on the street or found at taxi ranks near major attractions or transport hubs. Be sure to check that the taxi's meter is running to avoid overpaying.

Ride-Hailing: Services like Uber and Bolt operate in Paris and can be a good option if you're traveling to or from areas not well-served by public transport.

Money-Saving Tips for Paris

Paris is often considered one of the more expensive destinations in Europe, but there are plenty of ways to enjoy the City of Light without breaking the bank. From sightseeing to dining and shopping, you can experience all the beauty and culture of Paris on a budget. Here are some practical money-saving tips to help you make the most of your time in Paris without overspending.

1. Visit Free Attractions and Museums

Paris is home to a wealth of free attractions and museums that allow you to soak in the culture without spending a penny.

Free Museums and Exhibitions

Musée d'Art Moderne (Museum of Modern Art): Located in the 16th arrondissement, this museum offers free entry to its permanent collection of modern and contemporary art, including works by Picasso, Braque, and Duchamp.

Petit Palais: This elegant museum houses fine art collections and is free to visit, offering a peaceful escape from the crowds.

Musée Carnavalet: This museum dedicated to the history of Paris is free to visit and takes you through the city's fascinating past.

Free Landmarks and Parks

Notre-Dame Cathedral: While the tower and crypt require tickets, entry to the cathedral itself is free.

Luxembourg Gardens: A beautiful park located in the 6th arrondissement, perfect for a leisurely stroll or a picnic.

Parc des Buttes-Chaumont: One of Paris's largest parks, featuring waterfalls, caves, and sweeping views of the city, ideal for a relaxing afternoon.

Montmartre and Sacré-Cœur: Visiting the Sacré-Cœur Basilica and enjoying the views from the top of Montmartre is free.

2. Save on Transportation with Passes

Getting around Paris can be costly, but there are several passes and options that will save you money on transportation.

Metro and Bus Passes

Paris Visite Pass: This unlimited travel pass offers access to the metro, RER, buses, trams, and Montmartre funicular for 1, 2, 3, or 5 days. It's especially useful if you plan on using public transport frequently throughout the day.

Navigo Card: If you're staying in Paris for a week or more, the Navigo card offers unlimited travel on the metro, RER, buses, and trams within central Paris. It's a great deal for longer stays.

Vélib' Bike Rentals

The Vélib' bike-share system allows you to rent bikes for as little as €1.70 for a 30-minute ride. This is an affordable and enjoyable way to explore Paris, and the first 30 minutes are free with the regular pass.

3. Take Advantage of Free Walking Tours

A great way to learn about Paris without spending money is by joining free walking tours. These tours are often led by local guides who work on a tips-only basis, meaning you can enjoy a comprehensive tour and pay what you can afford.

Sandemans New Paris Tours: Offering free walking tours that cover popular areas like the Latin Quarter, Montmartre, and Le Marais, this is an excellent way to learn about the city's history and culture.

Paris Greeters: A free walking tour program where locals show visitors around their neighborhoods, providing a personal and authentic experience.

4. Eat Like a Local

Dining out in Paris can be expensive, but there are plenty of affordable options if you know where to look.

Eat at Bistros and Cafés

Prix Fixe Menus: Many bistros and cafés offer a prix fixe menu (fixed-price menu) for lunch or dinner, which typically includes an appetizer, main course, and dessert for a set price. These menus are a great way to try traditional French dishes at a more affordable rate.

Cafés and Brasseries: Opt for cafés or brasseries where you can enjoy a classic French meal without the hefty price tag of Michelin-starred restaurants. For example, many cafes offer affordable plat du jour (dish of the day) options.

Take Advantage of Bakeries

Baguettes and Pastries: Head to local bakeries (boulangeries) for freshly baked baguettes, croissants, and pastries, which are delicious and inexpensive. Many bakeries also sell sandwiches and quiches for a budget-friendly lunch option.

Picnic in the Park

For a more cost-effective and relaxed meal, visit local food markets and grocery stores to stock up on items like cheese, charcuterie, fruit, and baguettes. Enjoy your picnic in one of Paris's many beautiful parks like Tuileries Gardens or the Luxembourg Gardens.

5. Shop Smart

Paris is a shopper's paradise, but it's easy to get carried away. If you're looking to pick up some souvenirs or shop for fashion without blowing your budget, here are a few tips.

Shop at Local Markets

Marché aux Puces de Saint-Ouen: If you love antiques, head to this famous flea market in the northern part of Paris, where you can find everything from vintage clothing to unique homeware at reasonable prices.

Local Food Markets: Markets like Marché d'Aligre or Marché des Enfants Rouges offer fresh produce, cheeses, and more at reasonable prices, perfect for picking up some delicious, authentic Parisian ingredients for a picnic.

Outlet Shopping

La Vallée Village: Located just outside Paris, this outlet mall offers discounts of up to 33% on luxury brands like Prada, Burberry, and Coach. A great way to score high-end items at lower prices.

6. Free Events and Festivals

Paris hosts many free events and festivals throughout the year that allow you to experience its culture without spending a dime.

Paris Jazz Festival (Summer): Held in Parc Floral, this free jazz festival attracts talented musicians from around the world.

Fête de la Musique (June 21): On this day, live music performances fill the streets of Paris, and anyone can participate by performing or enjoying the free concerts.

Nuit Blanche (October): This all-night arts festival allows visitors to experience art installations and exhibitions throughout the city, all free of charge.

7. Use Discount Passes for Sights and Attractions

Many of Paris's top attractions offer discount passes for multiple visits or combination tickets that allow you to save on entry fees.

Museum Pass

The Paris Museum Pass gives you entry to over 50 museums and monuments, including the Louvre, Musée d'Orsay, and Notre-Dame. With this pass, you can skip the long lines and visit as many attractions as you like over 2, 4, or 6 days, making it a good value if you plan to visit several museums.

Paris Pass

The Paris Pass includes not only museum entry but also skip-the-line access to major sights and a hop-on, hop-off bus tour. It also covers public transport, making it an excellent choice for tourists who plan to explore extensively.

8. Book Attractions and Tickets in Advance

To avoid paying higher prices at the door, it's often cheaper to book tickets to attractions and tours in advance.

Skip the Lines: Many major attractions, such as the Eiffel Tower or the Louvre, offer discounted prices if you purchase tickets online. Plus, you'll avoid the long queues, saving both time and money.

Special Offers: Look out for promotional deals on various tourism websites or attraction-specific websites for discounted tickets or group deals.

Packing Essentials for Every Season in Paris

Paris is a city of diverse seasons, each offering a unique experience. Whether you're planning a winter escape or a summer getaway, it's important to pack the right essentials to ensure comfort while exploring the City of Light. Below is a comprehensive guide to packing for every season in Paris, keeping in mind the typical weather and activities you might encounter during your visit.

Spring (March - May)

Spring in Paris is a delightful time to visit. The weather is mild and the city's parks and gardens come alive with blooming flowers. However, the weather can be unpredictable, so it's important to be prepared for both sunny days and unexpected rain showers.

Packing Essentials for Spring:

Light Layers: The temperatures during spring can range from cool to warm, so it's best to pack layers. A lightweight jacket or trench coat will come in handy for the cooler mornings and evenings.

Umbrella or Rain Jacket: Paris experiences occasional spring showers, so packing a compact umbrella or a water-resistant jacket is a must to stay dry.

Comfortable Shoes: You'll be walking a lot, so comfortable, stylish shoes are key. A pair of waterproof sneakers or flats will serve you well, especially on rainy days.

Sunglasses: Even though it's spring, Paris can have plenty of sunny days. A good pair of sunglasses is essential for sightseeing in the sunshine.

Light Sweaters and Scarves: Parisian fashion includes scarves throughout the year. A light scarf can add both style and warmth when needed, and a sweater will help you stay cozy when temperatures dip.

Summer (June - August)

Summer in Paris brings warm temperatures, with highs often reaching the low 80s°F (26°C). It's an ideal time to enjoy the city's outdoor cafés, gardens, and boat rides along the Seine, but it can get quite hot, especially in July and August.

Packing Essentials for Summer:

Lightweight Clothing: Pack breathable fabrics such as cotton, linen, and silk to stay cool in the summer heat. A mix of skirts, dresses, shorts, and short-sleeve tops will ensure you stay comfortable.

Sun Protection: The Parisian sun can be strong in summer, so bring a wide-brimmed hat, sunscreen, and sunglasses to protect yourself from UV rays.

Comfortable Walking Shoes: You'll be walking through cobbled streets, parks, and museums. Opt for comfortable sandals or sneakers that offer support.

Light Jacket or Cardigan: While the days are warm, evenings can sometimes be cooler. Pack a lightweight jacket or cardigan for late-night strolls along the Seine.

Swimwear: If you plan to visit the public swimming pools or take a dip in the Seine, pack your swimsuit. Paris also has several beautiful spots for river cruises that may offer swimming.

Autumn (September - November)

Autumn in Paris brings cooler weather, with crisp mornings and nights, along with the beauty of fall foliage in the parks and gardens. The city sees fewer tourists in the fall, making it a great time for a peaceful and scenic experience.

Packing Essentials for Autumn:

Warm Layers: As temperatures begin to drop, pack sweaters, long-sleeve shirts, and a heavier coat for evenings. A lightweight wool or cashmere sweater is perfect for layering.

Scarves and Gloves: The chilly mornings and evenings will make scarves, gloves, and hats necessary, especially in late autumn.

Boots: Comfortable ankle or knee-high boots are perfect for the autumn months, providing warmth and style for navigating Parisian streets.

Rain Gear: Autumn in Paris is known for its rainy days. Be sure to pack a good umbrella or a waterproof jacket to stay dry during the occasional downpour.

Pants and Tights: Layer tights or leggings under skirts and dresses, or opt for long pants to stay warm on cooler days.

Winter (December - February)

Winter in Paris can be cold, especially in January and February. While it rarely snows, temperatures can drop to near freezing, and the air feels chilly. Paris is less crowded in winter, but the holiday season brings festive lights and markets that add to the city's charm.

Packing Essentials for Winter:

Heavy Coat or Down Jacket: A warm, insulated coat is essential for winter in Paris. Look for something stylish yet functional to navigate the cold temperatures.

Layered Clothing: Thermal tops, sweaters, and scarves will help you stay warm as you explore the city. Layering is key to adjusting to fluctuating temperatures.

Waterproof Footwear: Winter can bring damp and muddy conditions, especially in parks. Waterproof boots or shoes are important for keeping your feet dry.

Warm Accessories: A hat, gloves, and scarf are absolute must-haves to protect your extremities from the cold. Opt for wool or fleece-lined options for maximum warmth.

Thermal Socks and Layers: When temperatures dip, thermal socks and base layers will make all the difference in staying comfortable during your walks through the city.

Indoor Clothing for Relaxing: Even though you'll likely spend most of your time outside, bring comfortable indoor clothing like loungewear for evenings spent in cafés or cozy evenings at your hotel.

General Tips for Packing for Paris:

French Fashion Considerations: Parisians are known for their chic, minimalist style. You don't need to overpack or bring anything too flashy. Neutral colors, simple cuts, and high-quality items will make you blend in effortlessly with the fashionable locals.

Small Backpack or Crossbody Bag: While a rolling suitcase might be convenient for airport transfers, a small backpack or crossbody bag is ideal for day trips around the city. Paris is known for pickpockets, so opt for a secure, zipped bag.

Portable Power Bank: You'll be using your phone for navigation, photos, and tickets, so bring a portable power bank to keep your devices charged throughout the day.

Reusable Water Bottle: Stay hydrated while exploring by bringing a reusable water bottle. Tap water in Paris is safe to drink, and you'll save money by refilling your bottle at fountains around the city.

Safety Tips and Common Scams to Avoid in Paris

Paris is one of the most visited cities in the world, attracting millions of tourists each year. While the city offers incredible sights and experiences, it's important to be aware of safety tips and common scams that could affect your visit. This guide will help you navigate the streets of Paris confidently, ensuring that you can enjoy all the city has to offer without falling victim to common pitfalls.

General Safety Tips for Paris

1. Stay Aware of Your Surroundings:

Paris is generally safe for tourists, but like any major city, petty crime does occur. Stay alert, especially in crowded areas like metro stations, major attractions, and tourist hotspots.

Keep your personal belongings close to you and avoid distractions (such as looking at your phone or map in public places).

2. Use Reliable Transportation:

The Paris Métro (subway) is safe and efficient, but always be aware of pickpockets, especially during rush hour or when the train is crowded. Stand with your back against a wall to prevent someone from sneaking up behind you.

For taxis, always use licensed ones. You can hail a cab from the street or use reputable taxi apps. Avoid getting into unmarked cars.

3. Keep Your Belongings Secure:

Carry a small, crossbody bag or backpack with secure zippers. A money belt or neck pouch is a good option for valuables like passports, credit cards, and cash.

Avoid carrying large amounts of cash. Use a combination of credit cards and small amounts of euros for convenience.

4. Know Emergency Contacts:

In case of an emergency, dial 112 (European emergency number) for fire, police, or medical assistance.

The number for local police is 17, and you can reach an ambulance by dialing 15.

5. Protect Your Personal Information:

Be cautious when sharing personal information, especially over the phone or on public Wi-Fi networks. Use a VPN (Virtual Private Network) when accessing sensitive accounts on public Wi-Fi.

6. Stay in Well-Lit, Busy Areas at Night:

While Paris is relatively safe at night, it's best to avoid less-traveled streets, parks, or alleys. Stick to well-lit and busy areas, particularly when returning to your accommodation after dark.

Common Scams in Paris and How to Avoid Them

Despite Paris being a relatively safe city, there are several common scams that target tourists. Being aware of these scams can help you avoid unpleasant experiences.

1. The Friendship Bracelet Scam

How it Works: A person, often a woman or child, approaches you while you're walking or sitting in tourist-heavy areas (like near the Eiffel Tower or Sacré-Cœur). They will offer to make you a "friendship bracelet" or tie a string around your wrist. Once they do, they demand a large amount of money.

How to Avoid It: Politely refuse if anyone approaches you with such an offer. Don't let anyone touch you or your belongings, and walk away from the situation immediately.

2. The Petition Scam

How it Works: A person will approach you with a petition asking you to sign in support of a cause, such as helping disabled children or supporting a charity. Once you sign, they will insist that you donate money, sometimes with aggressive tactics.

How to Avoid It: Politely decline to sign any petitions, especially if they approach you on the street or in a tourist area. Walk away quickly if you feel pressured.

3. Pickpockets in Crowded Areas

How it Works: Pickpockets often target crowded areas like busy metro stations, markets, and tourist attractions. They may work in groups, using distractions such as someone spilling something on you, bumping into you, or asking for directions.

How to Avoid It: Be vigilant in crowded areas. Keep your bag or wallet in front of you, preferably in an anti-theft bag, and avoid putting your phone or wallet in your back pocket. If someone bumps into you or gets too close, check your belongings immediately.

4. Fake Charity Workers

How it Works: Scam artists posing as charity workers approach tourists, particularly near major attractions. They might show you a badge or a form claiming that they are raising money for a noble cause. They may insist on donations, even pressuring you to donate large sums.

How to Avoid It: If someone approaches you asking for donations or money for a charity, do not engage or give money. Legitimate charity workers will not pressure you into giving and are often registered with official organizations.

5. The "Lost Ring" Scam

How it Works: Someone will drop a ring in front of you, and when you pick it up, they will claim it belongs to them and demand money for it. In some cases, they will offer to sell the ring to you for a low price.

How to Avoid It: If you see a ring or any other item on the ground, ignore it. If someone approaches you claiming it's theirs, walk away and avoid any interaction.

6. Taxi Scams

How it Works: Some unlicensed taxi drivers may approach you at airports or busy train stations offering rides. They might charge exorbitant fees, use a non-metered fare, or take you on a longer route to increase the fare.

How to Avoid It: Always use official, licensed taxis. Book taxis in advance through a reputable app or at an official taxi stand. Ensure that the meter is running and confirm the price before you get in.

7. The "Broken Camera" Scam

How it Works: A person will ask you to take their picture or offer to take your picture. While doing so, they will pretend that your camera or phone is broken, asking for money to fix it.

How to Avoid It: Be cautious when someone offers to take your picture. If you're in a public place, it's safer to ask a fellow tourist to take the photo instead. Never hand over your camera or phone to strangers.

8. The Fake Ticket Scam

How it Works: Scammers may sell fake tickets for attractions, concerts, or events, often near popular tourist sites. They might claim that the tickets are sold out or that they have a "special deal" for tourists.

How to Avoid It: Purchase tickets directly from official websites, authorized resellers, or ticket offices. Avoid buying tickets from street vendors or unauthorized individuals.

How to Stay Safe:

1. Use Trusted Apps for Maps and Transportation:

Download official transportation apps such as RATP for public transit or Uber for taxis to ensure reliable and safe transport options.

2. Secure Your Hotel Room:

Use the hotel safe to store your valuables when you're out. Double-check that windows and doors are locked before leaving your room, and avoid leaving your room key unattended.

3. Trust Your Instincts:

If something doesn't feel right or if someone is pressuring you, trust your instincts and walk away. Paris is generally safe, but being cautious and aware of your surroundings can prevent unwanted situations.

Index

Made in the USA
Las Vegas, NV
17 January 2025

16535238R00083